Putting Our
DIFFERENCES
to WORK

Putting Our DIFFERENCES to WORK

The Fastest Way to Innovation, Leadership, and High Performance

Debbe Kennedy

Foreword by Joel A. Barker

BK

Berrett–Koehler Publishers, Inc.
San Francisco
a BK Business book

Berrett-Koehler Publishers, Inc.
235 Montgomery Street, Suite 650
San Francisco, CA 94104-2916
Tel: (415) 288-0260   Fax: (415) 362-2512   www.bkconnection.com

Ordering Information

Quantity sales. Special discounts are available on quantity purchases by corporations, associations, and others. For details, contact the "Special Sales Department" at the Berrett-Koehler address above.

Individual sales. Berrett-Koehler publications are available through most bookstores. They can also be ordered directly from Berrett-Koehler: Tel: (800) 929-2929; Fax: (802) 864-7626; www.bkconnection.com

Orders for college textbook/course adoption use. Please contact Berrett-Koehler: Tel: (800) 929-2929; Fax: (802) 864-7626.

Orders by U.S. trade bookstores and wholesalers. Please contact Ingram Publisher Services, Tel: (800) 509-4887; Fax: (800) 838-1149; E-mail: customer.service@ingrampublisherservices.com; or visit www.ingrampublisherservices.com/Ordering for details about electronic ordering.

Production Management: Michael Bass Associates
Cover Design and Illustrations: Sally K. Green
Copyeditor: Laura Larson
Book Design: Linda M. Robertson

Library of Congress Cataloging-in-Publication Data
  Kennedy, Debbe.
    Putting our differences to work : the fastest way to innovation, leadership, and high performance / by Debbe Kennedy.—1st ed.
      p. cm.
    Includes bibliographical references and index.
    ISBN 978-1-57675-499-3 (hardcover : alk. paper)
    1. Diversity in the workplace. 2. Teams in the workplace. 3. Leadership.
  4. Problem solving. 5. Decision-making. 6. Organizational effectiveness. I. Title.
    HF5549.5.M5K46 2008
    658.3008—dc22
                                                                    2008011589

First Edition
13 12 11 10 09 08   10 9 8 7 6 5 4 3 2 1

This book is dedicated to

Johanna
Andrew
Samantha
Austin
Kassie
Jake

and to
YOU

and other leaders
and innovators
everywhere

Contents

PART 3

EVER-EXPANDING POSSIBILITIES 151

Foreword

by Joel A. Barker

For centuries people assumed that economic growth resulted from the interplay between capital and labor. Today we know that these elements are outweighed by a single critical factor: innovation. Innovation is the source of U.S. economic leadership and the foundation for our competitiveness in the global economy.

That's what Bill Gates wrote in the *Washington Post* in early 2007. Without a doubt, leaders around the world understand the leverage of innovation and want a share in the wealth it creates.

Debbe Kennedy has written a book that approaches innovation leadership in a unique way. It focuses on the power of bringing differences together to create new products, services, and new levels of contribution. It is based on her work of the last fifteen years, and every idea has been tested and proven. In a world in which diversity is becoming more important every day, knowing how to use that diversity for innovation is a huge competitive advantage. That's what *Putting Our Differences to Work* offers.

Debbe has developed and refined three themes she uses to create the change that results in increased innovation:

Theme 1. The world and your organization are getting more diverse so you must understand how to deal with diversity at all levels—in the boardroom, in the organization, in the field, in the marketplace.

Theme 2. Leading a diverse organization is very different from leading an organization with high homogeneity. Twenty-first-century leadership is going to be about leading diverse followers. Those who can apply "diversity leadership" have a huge advantage over those who cannot.

Theme 3. If you know how to utilize diversity, you can rapidly reap continuous benefits in innovation—both internal innovations that will make your organization better, and external innovations that your customers will clamor for.

ix

What Debbe has done is create a series of easy-to-follow guidelines, instructions, and suggestions for your organization—and every leader in it—on how to utilize diversity to increase innovation. Every one of her ideas has been tested by her in multiple settings. She's also included a special section referencing key studies, tools, and other resources for you to do your own explorations.

She has simple strategies that work for organizations of all sizes. She has thoughtful guidelines for dealing with the people issues and the "Not in my backyard" issues. And she has wonderful stories of success told by the "succeeders" in their own words.

And scattered throughout her book are wise observations, some two thousand years old, some fresh off the Internet. They illustrate the depth of thinking and experience that has gone into this book.

While *Putting Our Differences to Work* has something for everyone, it is particularly important for those who would be leaders. Debbe pulls no punches about how bad leadership behavior in a diverse world dramatically damages an organization's ability to innovate. But, after pointing out the bad behavior, she offers clear, thoughtful instructions on how to overcome the past and develop a leadership style fit for the twenty-first century.

This is a book that you will read and then find yourself going back to again and again, to access its many ideas on innovation, on leadership, and on productivity that results from good leadership and constant innovation.

It will change the way you think about diversity. It will show you how to leverage diversity. It will help you become a better leader.

What I like best about *Putting Our Differences to Work* is that Debbe teaches us how diversity accelerates innovation to everyone's advantage. This is a win-win-win book in which you and your people win, your organization wins, and the world wins.

Joel Barker
Futurist, filmmaker, author
Paradigms: The Business of Discovering the Future

Note: Also see Chapter 10, "Innovation at the Verge of Differences," by Joel Barker.

"Out of clutter find simplicity; from discord find harmony; in the middle of difficulty lies opportunity."

—Albert Einstein

Preface

Do you ever feel like the whole world is looking to you for leadership—even if it's just your own world? Today we find ourselves in similar places regardless of our business or organization. The pressures are on. Demands for new ideas and new talent are real. Growth seems to be on everyone's mind, whether it is to grow your business, expand your influence, multiply your supporters, increase your diverse talent pool, or gain market share. And, by the way, make it fast.

A respected leader once shared with me that the word *leadership* has a Germanic origin meaning to "find a new path." What is encouraging amid all the chaos today is there is a constant stream of achievements rising up from individuals and organizations across the world *finding new paths* that are creatively addressing the problems we face with new thinking and a resurgence of our pioneering spirit as people.

I wrote this book for you to experience walking on some of those new paths and, at the same time, take away everything you need to forge your own. The idea for this book arose out of observation, experience, participation, and inspiration from what seems a lifetime of study and practice that has involved *putting our differences to work*. The most meaningful part of the journey has come from those I met and learned from and with along the way. Writing the book grew out of first asking myself a number of new questions, and now I ask you to consider them, too:

- ▶ Who needs to become a leader today?
- ▶ What skills and qualities do we really need in our leaders at all levels?
- ▶ What role do people and their differences play in our achievements?
- ▶ How well are we utilizing the talent we have?
- ▶ If innovation is the "engine of growth," what fuels the engine?

▶ Where is the greatest opportunity for innovation?

▶ How can everyone contribute and reap the benefits of innovation?

The answers to these questions hold the promise of healing, enriching, and transforming workplaces, marketplaces, communities, and our world, and they formed the premise of *Putting Our Differences to Work*. The ideas in this practical guide change the prevailing rules of how to think, behave, and operate as leaders and innovators in three specific ways.

First, we learn that all we already know about leadership is valuable. However, to strengthen our portfolio of skills, five distinctive qualities of leadership are introduced. They fundamentally change the rules in how we think and act. They reframe old notions that no longer work to our advantage in our organizations or wherever we find ourselves having an opportunity to have a positive influence on others. These qualities are needed at all levels of leadership, including individual contributors and aspiring leaders who may not see themselves as leaders. Our distributed workplaces and communities mean that we all step in and out of leadership roles that require new skills to understand, interact, and relate with others different than we are.

Second, the ideas in this book draw together four diverse elements of business and society that have traditionally been handled separately in our work and our thinking—if not by our words and processes, then certainly by our visible actions and practices: *innovation, leadership, diversity*, and *inclusion*. *Putting Our Differences to Work* reframes how these four elements are connected and proves the possibilities that reside with this powerful foursome. The outcome is measurable with meaningful benefits for individuals, business, society, and our world.

Third, the ideas in the book elevate the significance and importance of people. They put people and all their differences at the forefront of all achievement. We need them—and all of their differences, talents, energy, new ideas, and expertise. Diverse people are the fundamental fuel for innovation to serve business and society, for new levels of leadership in our respective fields, and for realizing the highest levels of achievement for our organizations. Through concrete examples, you will learn how our differences multiply the possibilities for innovation, the "engine of growth." You will also witness the profound influence that inclusion has to engage everyone, accelerating the process of acceptance, understanding, and ownership for new ideas, as well as new products and services. The ideas in this book ask us to reconsider where we are today and reach beyond the trendy economic jargon that has come into fashion that defines people in terms of *human capital* and tends to overlook the importance of people considerations in the mainstream of our business and organizational strategies.

Everything about this book, from its cover to its content, reflects the results of putting our differences to work. Its pages are marked with many fingerprints. I wanted it to be a book that reflected its title—a true mirror of putting our differences to work. This book holds the wisdom of many thought leaders, mentors, sages, and teachers crossing all segments of society. I've had the good fortune to know many of them. Some I've never met, but they are very present in this book. When all the differences are put together, it is a virtual gathering of great minds and pioneering spirits coming together across time and distance to share knowledge and know-how with you.

Every action taken in the process of writing this book brought with it echoing voices from all those who dreamed, dared, and sacrificed before us. I've heard them whispering across time as I worked on this book. Like all those with a pioneering spirit, one learns that history doesn't record every name and face, but all of us benefit today from the many who cared and risked and reached inside to find the strength to respond to the call of their generation and time.

Above my desk, seven original paintings stretch across my wall—of Mother Teresa, Viktor Frankl, Martin Luther King Jr., Nelson Mandela, Mahatma Gandhi, Jalaluddin Rumi, and Eleanor Roosevelt. Each face watches over me as I work every day, creating an ever-present reminder of the importance of this journey of continuous renewal that you and I are on at this time in history. I've always believed that we can remain in a continual dialogue with leaders like these shining examples if we are open to listen and learn from the wisdom they left for us.

While writing, I heard Dr. King reminding us once again why our efforts have significance: "All life is inter-related. We are all caught in an inescapable network of mutuality, tied into a single garment of destiny. Whatever affects one directly, affects all indirectly." Mother Teresa encourages us to step up and do our part: "Don't wait for the leaders. Do it alone, person to person." Gandhi inspires us when we are personally overwhelmed by the magnitude of the struggle: "When you are after a righteous cause, people pop out of the pavement to help you." Viktor Frankl doesn't let us escape without recognizing that regardless of how difficult and impossible circumstances may appear, we are in charge: "Everything can be taken from a man but...the last of the human freedoms—to choose one's attitude in any given set of circumstances, to choose one's way." Eleanor Roosevelt tests the authenticity of our leadership: "It is not fair to ask of others to do what you are unwilling to do yourself." Rumi reminds us, on many levels, that this is not a journey of thoughtless action: "Attention to small details, makes perfect a large work." And Nelson Mandela reminds us that "with freedom comes responsibility."

I learned long ago that a story is a moment in time you can revisit over and over again. Better yet, if the story contains wisdom and knowledge, it is timeless. Stories can ignite your courage. They can be a catalyst for a new idea. They can bring out the best in your leadership. When I was selecting the "pearls and gems" from my work to include in this book, there were special stories I wanted to share because they had this kind of enduring quality. Each story includes the context and my experience of the leaders. This seemed to bring life into each story that would be somehow lost, if not mentioned.

My greatest hope for *Putting Our Differences to Work* is that it will be one of those books that you read, internalize, put into practice, and keep as a ready reference and guide for using your passions, intellect, knowledge, and skill to pioneer a new era—one that puts your signature on the twenty-first century—opening the way for the human dimension of leadership to reign.

And now the journey begins.

May the returns for your efforts and example in putting our differences to work leave an enduring imprint wherever you are called to lead the way.

I welcome you.

Debbe Kennedy
Montara, California
April 2008

Introduction

The Fastest Way

Organizations and individuals all over the world are discovering that putting our differences to work is the most powerful accelerator for generating new ideas, creating innovative solutions, executing organizational strategies, and engaging everyone in the process.

This book is about how to make your own discovery of this truth. It comes with everything you need to get started right where you are.

The breakthrough is the essential ingredient of diversity, in its broadest sense. Real value lies at the intersection of our differences. This encompasses everything from our thinking styles, problem-solving approaches, experiences, competencies, work habits, and management styles to our ethnic origins, cultural backgrounds, and generational insight (see the Dimensions of Difference illustration). All our differences give each of us a unique perspective from which to draw, including gender, race, physical abilities, sexual orientation, nationality, religion, age, and everything that makes us who we are

Dimensions of Difference
The value lies at the intersection of all that makes us different...

1

as individuals. The magic begins when we come together. The secret is learning how, when, and where to tap into all the wealth of insight, wisdom, and new thinking to solve problems, create new products and services, and build stronger communities with benefits for everyone.

In 2005, I had an opportunity to get a memorable glimpse into our emerging generation of innovators and the experience of putting our differences to work today. I was invited to speak at an online Leadership Forum hosted by Microsoft on the topic of "How to Get Buy-in for New Ideas." With innovation commonly being known as "the engine of growth," I wasn't too surprised when the Forum drew a crowd. In what seemed an instant, over 550 leaders showed up online. I had no idea at the time that the group was so diverse, because I could only see their names. Later, I learned they came from over twenty countries representing regions across the world, including Europe, Asia Pacific, Canada, Latin America, and the United States, demonstrating that people with new ideas are a universal treasure. They represented major companies from every industry, as well as entrepreneurs, government, military, education, health care, and community organizations. I discovered the group was a cross section of CEOs and senior leaders, managers of every type, as well as educators, business owners, ministers, and consultants. Imagine all this diverse talent coming together, peer to peer, meeting on common ground, because we were brimming with new ideas to bring to our respective organizations. Up front, I asked the group why they came to this particular session. I admit, I was moved by the responses. I recognized there was a deeper level of connection among us that would have been missed if I hadn't asked the question. Ninety percent described themselves as change leaders or innovators with new ideas to improve their businesses and organizations. Nearly half indicated that, over and above their jobs, they had come because they hoped to change the world. And this was just a small random sampling of leaders at one meeting. I have learned, since this group heightened my own awareness, a growing number of us would describe ourselves and our missions in a similar way.

In this one hour, we accomplished much together. We learned about presenting new ideas and pinpointed common problems standing in the way of innovation, change, and growth in our organizations. The dialogue continued through emails and influenced a series of smaller online conversations that I hosted in the following weeks.

Three main issues generated the most comments, discussion, and correspondence afterward. They are indicators of the gaps that still exist between leaders and employees effectively putting their differences to work to innovate and influence organizational success. See if any of these sound familiar to you and what other truths you might add to the mix from your own experience:

- ▶ Our company culture isn't open to new ideas; process is more important. There is a lack of interest in change and innovation. Everyone sees the need; no one wants to take the risk. New approaches aren't welcomed.
- ▶ Gender, race, and age still play a role in acceptance of new ideas in our organization. If you think differently or ask too many questions, it leads to losing the respect of senior leaders.
- ▶ Senior leaders/managers take ideas and present them as their own. The focus from our leaders is on execution of strategy; they've forgotten people are leading it for them. It would be great if they showed more interest in what people have to say.

These comments are good examples of common issues that stand in the way of putting our differences to work effectively across any organization. This kind of breakdown in communication erodes trust and impacts productivity and achievement in ways we may not even notice unless we are paying attention. Here is a question to consider for yourself and your organization:

What are the chances you or other leaders in your organization might be leaving similar impressions with those looking to you for leadership?

Most of us go along thinking we are doing a great job, so receiving this kind of feedback isn't fun, often comes as a surprise—never at a good time—and is disappointing to the best of us. No one would purposely want to have members of their teams thinking this way. The important lesson we all need to remember is directly related to effectively putting our differences to work: it isn't what we think we are doing that matters; it isn't what we've said, think we've said, or wish we'd said; it is what others perceive and receive from us that has the sweeping influences—influences we often don't realize restrict both the individuals and the organization from delivering the highest levels of results, innovation, leadership, and performance.

One of our biggest culprits is our language. Putting our differences to work requires that we develop the ability to communicate with the people we are counting on most to fulfill our business and organizational strategies and goals. This means reaching them, understanding what they need from us to be great themselves, so they can accomplish great things for the

Top 10 CEO Challenges Overall
Rankings of Challenges of "Greatest Concern"

---

1. Excellence in execution
2. Sustained and steady top-line growth
3. Consistent execution of strategy by top management
4. Profit growth
5. Finding qualified managerial talent
6. Customer loyalty and retention
7. Speed, flexibility, adaptability to change
8. Corporate reputation
9. Stimulating innovation/ creativity/enabling entrepreneurship
10. Speed to market

Source: The Conference Board, October 2007.

organization. To do this, we need to become conscious of what we say and how we say it.

Eric Hoffer, a well-known American social writer, summed up this need nicely: "The leader has to be practical and a realist, yet must talk the language of the visionary and the idealist." In recent years, "the visionary and the idealist" messages that come from a leader's heart are frequently getting replaced with economic buzz words in sound-byte form. One example of this trend shows up in the results of a survey.

In October 2007, The Conference Board released its CEO Top 10 Challenges, reporting the results of a survey of 769 global CEOs from 40 countries. Each of these challenges is largely dependent on the commitment, ingenuity, brainpower, grit, and new ideas of the *people* behind them. But would you know people were important by the way these concerns are expressed? People were not mentioned as one of the "greatest concerns." Unfortunately, many of these "people-less" words and expressions become our talking points—and we wonder why people don't feel more energized, inspired, and engaged. Those of us who can most effectively eliminate inhibitors to putting differences to work within our teams and organizations will have a decided advantage because we will have developed new mindsets and skill sets about communicating with our people to support our success.

This book is a practical guide for leaders at all levels. It is designed to support any organization's challenges by bringing out the best in everyone. It comes packed with knowledge, know-how, and inspiration to help you more effectively put differences to work. It establishes the need for change, offers real-to-life stories to prove its premise, and defines five distinctive qualities of leadership to lead the way. To help you map a goal-directed journey, it includes a well-defined process with six action steps, best practices, and both strategic and tactical ideas to foster your thinking and actions in making differences the catalyst for new thinking, new approaches, and new contributions that will serve business and society.

In a kind of paradox, I must admit the idea of putting our differences to work isn't a trendy new concept. There is nothing trendy about it. It is steeped in substance. History is replete with examples that cover every kind of human experience in work and life, yet we still struggle with it.

In recent years, on many fronts, I think it's safe to say that our confidence, our capacity, and our capability have been shaken. We've lost touch with the power we have when we join together, because opportunities to demonstrate it have been moved into the background amid lots of churn and pressures of doing more with less. In most cases, putting our differences to work has been unintentionally shadowed by an ever-increasing demand for the leader's mind share and a time of massive change in the very nature of how we work and live.

What we may have forgotten is that we've proven over and over again that we know how to put our differences to work. In fact, this book has over twenty-five present-day stories demonstrating many of its lessons, qualities, and best practices in action. I'm certain, as you read the stories, you will be reminded of similar experiences you've had or stories with a little different twist. As I write, I've had my own flashbacks.

My first recollection of experiencing the power of putting our differences to work came in my first year as a new manager at IBM. How I got there was a story all its own that sets the stage.

I had a hip, metropolitan life in Los Angeles, California, where I worked at IBM's landmark high-rise on Wilshire Boulevard. I had been with IBM for five years at the time. I visited Alaska on vacation late that summer and stopped by the IBM office. To my surprise, they offered me a job. In what seemed a flash, I accepted and boldly moved to what seemed, at the time, a foreign land: Anchorage, Alaska, a new business frontier.

I arrived in the dead of winter. I worked in IBM's shoddy two-story building with old rusted-out desks and a broken elevator. The view from my new office was a far cry from the bustle of the well-groomed business district I was used to in L.A. Instead, it was a landscape devoid of any colors, except brown and white. It became an ever-present symbol of the drastic change before me. On my desk I kept my welcoming gift, a local book entitled *Life without Lettuce*. It was different all right—a pioneering journey of sorts. The job called upon me to adapt fast, be flexible, focused, and get fired up in this new uncharted territory.

In a short time, in stark contrast to the exterior brown and white landscape, I felt a vibrant energy inside this uncommon workplace. It was fun and full of life with a cast of characters you would never imagine working side by side. Because most of us had been imported from other places, we had no families nearby. It was indeed a melting pot.

We enjoyed the rewards of being the top revenue-producing office in the country in our division; topping all the charts, and getting lots of attention. In a short time, I was promoted to my first manager job, which put me among the first women managers at IBM in the northwest United States. The leadership team that I joined consisted of all men—most of whom could be described as the rough, gruff, rugged, earthy, bush pilot types.

After just four hours as a manager, we were all summoned into a makeshift conference room. The "big boss" from the "lower 48" had flown into town unannounced, and he didn't look happy. He was the last to enter the room. I still remember how he slammed the door shut, and I recall his exact words: "All indications are that this is a failed corporate audit." The news shocked me. It was the first time I realized it was possible to be one of the best offices and also one of the most out of control and not realize it. Our mission was then explained: we were to turn the place around if we were all to survive.

Survive we did—in a big way. We involved everyone. Many of us were called to work outside the comfort zones of our own jobs. We tapped into our differences, creatively calling upon diverse thinking styles, problem-solving skills, cultural knowledge, and even expertise in traveling to remote villages. For the most complex issues, we hand-picked the people on the team with a track record for knowing how to solve problems, instead of simply relying on our obvious experts who might be blinded by their own processes and methods, some of which had proven faulty in the audit. Top salesmen teamed with our all-women accounts receivable staff to use their clout, influence, and charm to collect huge sums of money long past due. Our rough and rugged "bush pilots," familiar with the cultures in the back country of Alaska, partnered with sales and service, hopping in their planes to solve problems at remote customer sites. Technical support people aided those in charge of security to figure out how to better secure the building and the company's assets. Administrative assistants were turned into analysts, responsible for establishing new business controls. I can still see our branch manager sitting in the "bullpen," answering phones when it was necessary.

In a matter of months, with a lot of hard work, we were not only a top revenue-producing office but also one of the top operating organizations. Our team was recognized for its dedication to mission and innovative approach; our heroes were rewarded.

The following spring, I was promoted to a regional job in Seattle where I began helping other leaders work with their organizations to put differences to work to solve complex organizational problems. Much to my surprise, a few months into my new job, I was named Manager of the Year for my contributions in Alaska. I mention this only to point out the power and enduring influence leaders have on their people. What I've never forgotten is the character they demonstrated to me as a young leader. You see, because I had already moved on to a new assignment, consideration for this honor could have easily been pushed aside—you know, "out of sight; out of mind." In fact, I've always known that choosing another manager for this honor certainly would have been more advantageous for the two managers making the decision. I recently read somewhere that one of the most profound tests of your character as a leader is the way you treat people who can no longer directly benefit you. The message made me think of Joe and Gerry, the two leaders involved. I don't know where they are today, but not only did they teach me how to put differences to work and reward them; they also set a standard of leadership conduct and integrity that left an enduring imprint on me in the years that followed.

The lessons that came from that adventure in Alaska started with my life and work being turned upside down by change. I learned much from our unlikely team with many *differences*—a motley group who found themselves stuck with one another in an unexpected twist of fate with a critical mission to *move mountains*, solving the unsolvable in record time.

Much has changed in the world since then. Looking back, the story looks like just a good example of teamwork, doesn't it? Perhaps at the time, "good teamwork" is all we could see in such an experience—maybe all we needed to see. Putting our differences to work at the level needed today asks much more of us than the obvious, seemingly commonplace attributes of teamwork and considerations of diversity, inclusion, and change that pop out in my Alaska story.

Putting our differences to work takes all we've learned about teamwork to a whole new level. It requires us to become skilled at working together across a broader spectrum of dimensions of diversity, as well as distance with precision, speed, and agility. Moreover, technology continues to reshape how, when, and where we connect, challenging us to remain open and trusting of the unknown and different.

We've fast-forwarded to a whole new workplace reality with few boundaries. Our environments are no longer traditional workplaces, and diversity is now a reality. We're having to learn how to put our goals and shared values into the melting pot of the common good in order to creatively address the problems we have to solve together. In every direction, the problems for business and society call for not only the mind of a leader but the hearts and the consciences of each person.

The demand for leaders with increased knowledge, skills, and conscious people-focused habits is ever-rising as we move further into the twenty-first century. When you look around at the existing turmoil and uncertainty in the marketplaces, workplaces, and communities throughout the world, there is a sense of urgency about this need.

As I've witnessed and experienced this need in my own work, a repeated echo of wisdom, shared with me in the final days of the twentieth century comes back to me often. In what seemed a by-chance occasion at just the right time, I had the honor to meet Lieutenant General David H. Ohle, then deputy chief of staff for personnel for the United States Army at a special gathering at the Leader to Leader Institute (formerly the Peter F. Drucker Foundation) in New York. General Ohle was accompanied by a couple of officers from his leadership team. I admit that I was a bit surprised to discover the common challenges we shared as leaders and the common solutions we were all seeking. Before the evening ended, the general invited me to spend a day with him and his leadership team at the Pentagon in Washington, D.C.

During our interview, he summed up the challenge for us as individuals and organizations of all kinds. "We are all going to have to move into the future in a new context," he told me. "For any organization, I think the next business revolution is conquering the human dimension of change. We need to bring leader development, training, and quality care for our people forward, so it matches what we have accomplished in creating more efficient, prosperous, and flatter organizations. For some time, we all have been captivated by the books on reengineering, downsizing, and restructuring, and we have done a terrific job applying what we have learned—innovating with technology, transforming organizations, and changing policies—but many of us, perhaps unintentionally, forgot about the people."

This book is also about shaping the future, and it comes with a personal invitation to *you* to join me and other leaders in pioneering a new era marked by mastery of putting our differences to work. The opportunity for each of us, and all of us, is to distinguish the twenty-first century as a time where, through the strength of our differences across the world, new levels of meaningful and useful innovation are realized, transforming business and society.

This may seem a lofty goal, but isn't that the role of leadership—to paint the picture of the future for those who follow us? By claiming this goal, we are destined to leave enduring fingerprints on the beginning of the century. Futurist Joel Barker points out what we have at stake: *You can and should shape your own future, because if you don't, someone else surely will.*

HOW THIS BOOK IS ORGANIZED

Because this book combines the power of first-person storytelling, knowledge, and wisdom, past and present, with that of being an enduring practical guide with tools and resources, I want to add a few comments about its design to guide your reading.

This book is divided into three parts. Part 1, "Taking Your Leadership to a New Level," is about the need for change, the leadership behaviors that will lead to success, and a few quick reference tools designed to support your work. It helps you look closely at not only what "putting our differences to work" means but what you already know about it, and what else you need to know as a leader. It points to why a more people-conscious leadership is important today from the perspective of prominent thought leaders and invites you to experience the evidence through the power of stories that prove it works.

Additionally, Part 1 introduces *Five Distinctive Qualities of Leadership* essential for putting our differences to work. Each is defined with key behaviors and actions to help you adapt and integrate them as part of your day-to-day leadership practice. This part also introduces *The Basics*, a set of tools and principles for success to guide your own personal journey of leadership development and renewal. You will be introduced to two helpful tools. First is the Putting Our Differences to Work: Six Steps That Make It Happen model, which shows how phases of change work together to achieve success. Second, the Organizational Snapshot is a simple online and downloadable assessment tool to test your team's or organization's readiness. It assists you in creating a reference point to mark where you are starting and in measuring your progress along the way.

Part 2, "Knowledge and Know-how to Guide the Way," is designed to be an enduring reference for you to navigate your way through each phase of change in putting differences to work. This six-step model is the road map. A separate chapter is dedicated to each unique and interrelated step: *Assessment, Acceptance, Action, Accountability, Achievement*, and *More Action*. Each of these six chapters provides an overview, first-person accounts, and wisdom from luminaries, as well as illustrative examples. Periodically throughout the book and following the stories, I have summarized key points to take away as well as ideas for putting the learning into practice.

Part 3, "Ever-Expanding Possibilities," is about moving beyond the basics and looking to the future. By invitation, Chapter 10, "Innovation at the Verge of Differences," is written by futurist Joel Barker. He introduces new discoveries affirming the link between diversity and innovation that have been the basis for our collaborative work since 2000. In Chapter 11, "Collaboration at the Verge of Differences," I relate our personal story of mutualistic collaboration with our respective teams and partners, sharing lessons learned. Chapter 12, "The Power of the Virtual Gathering Place," also offers a unique opportunity to look inside the expanding possibilities for the role of social networking and other Web 2.0 technologies that are bringing us ever closer to one another in different ways. Trailblazing leaders join me to share success stories and lessons learned in this new frontier in virtual space.

THE FASTEST WAY TO BEGIN

So what's the fastest way to begin putting our differences to work? The answer comes from a simple truth shared with me years ago.

On my first day of our new business, I asked a trusted friend and successful entrepreneur, "What's the fastest way to begin?" "Well," she said, looking at me straight on, "you get up in the morning and you *start.*" In the years since, I've realized the power of this simple truth over and over again in my work and my personal life. It is not only the fastest way to begin a business, but it is also the fastest way to begin a new era, to lead a new mission, to solve any problem, to change behavior, to transform an organization, or to seize any opportunity standing before you. *You just begin.* You may not know exactly what's ahead, but there is only one way to find out: Go! Move. Jump. Leap. Open the door and *enter.* It is that first forward-thinking step that holds the promise of a new and different future, as well as the spark of innovation, the influence of leadership, the power of a new more collaborative team or community, or the passion that leads to high performance. Across the world, in big and small ways, we're learning and relearning that when lots of individual leaders step up to take that initial bold move together, the creative possibilities multiply many times, producing results one could only describe as remarkable.

So, are you ready to get started? Come along with me as we begin taking leadership to the next level by putting our differences to work.

PART I

Taking Your Leadership to a New Level

"It is not the mountain we conquer but ourselves."

—Sir Edmund Hillary
New Zealand mountain climber and Antarctic Explorer
First to successfully climb Mount Everest

Taking one's leadership to a new level challenges the best of us. If you are like the leaders and innovators I know, unless we get a chance to slip away to attend a class or a conference or take a long-needed vacation, the demands of life and work leave little time to think about such personal renewal. However, this is a time in our organizations and in the world that requires something different from us all. A new world, an ever-changing reality is sounding its call to leaders at all levels. We are being asked to prove what we can do, what one of my mentors once called "changing our spots." We need to rethink where we are, how we act, where we need to go, and how we're going to get there. Part 1 is designed to get you started.

To set the stage for Part 1 and the chapters that follow, I have chosen a personal story to begin this part of our journey, knowing it will be a relevant theme throughout the rest of the book.

I am a hiker. I say this with a great sense of accomplishment as it didn't come naturally to me. Knowing we've all had our mountains to climb in work and life, it seems certain you will relate even if your mountains have been of a different nature. There are many parallels in my story about learning to hike a mountain and taking your leadership to a new level. The process of raising your capability, capacity, knowledge, and know-how in order to reap the benefits of diversity, accelerate innovation, and boost productivity requires a similar learning curve. As you read it, think about the experiences you've had that asked you to reach inside to grow.

I went on my first hike about ten years ago. It was a new beginning that stretched me mentally, emotionally, and physically. It was an awakening about the world around me. The outdoors was a foreign place at the time. Up to that point, my life and work had been so filled with making my way and surviving that I hadn't even taken the time to consciously notice that trees came in many varieties and mountains had paths upward with vistas that would become a catalyst for new visions, new contributions, and a sense of becoming more.

At first, I was clumsy, and everything about the experience felt awkward and unfamiliar. I had to retrain my thinking and beliefs to conquer even the first mountain peak. The journey required new skills, new tools, new discipline, and new habits. I had to reframe my flair for independence, joining in an interdependent collaboration with two friends, who were dramatically unique in every way. Our collective knowledge, focus, capability, agility, and adaptability were essential to forging unknown trails; each of us found our place to take the lead. We learned that it was our differences that generated safety, well-being, and the shared accomplishment of reaching the top. We learned like trees that grow on the ridge of a mountain, battered by the wind; like them, we, too, gained inner strength as we ascended.

In Part 1, we'll begin the climb of leadership renewal.

In Chapter 1, you'll have a chance to explore the need for change, as well as the what, why, and how of the new business essentials for putting our differences to work. Included are the findings of recent studies, as well as two extraordinary stories that respond to the question "So who says putting our differences to work is the fastest way?"

In Chapter 2, the focus is on introducing the Five Distinctive Qualities of Leadership. Here's where our paradigm gets shifted with five behavior-based qualities that fundamentally change how we think and operate as leaders and innovators, while using what we already know.

Chapter 3 includes the road map, compass, and necessary gear—the Basics. It walks through the process, introduces tools, and offers principles for success to guide your way.

CHAPTER I

The New Business Essentials

We don't have to look too far to see the pattern that has emerged in recent years showing our own struggles as leaders when it comes to putting differences to work effectively in our organizations. As cutting-edge global, market-driven strategies have become essential, it is clear that we, perhaps unintentionally, lost our focus on "people being our greatest assets." As we've worked to adapt to a changing world, the best of organizations have proven for a time that they are skilled at creating comprehensive worldwide business plans, launching a new strategic direction, blowing everyone away with innovative products or services, and compiling the financials that prove their worth. However, at the same time, *behind the scenes*, deep within the day-to-day operations, we also see genuine concern for people who slip into obscurity.

So how has this happened? Why do we continually struggle to keep a focus on people and putting differences to work, when there are such great benefits? Many would instantly argue that organizations and their leaders today are widely driven by their measures—the short-term bottom line, not what they do with people. True. Others would admit that many leaders focus on what they know how to do, especially when the demands to produce are ever-increasing and people leadership generally isn't a core skill for everyone. So we easily revert to what's familiar—the numbers and processes we can handle. We learned about them in school. We've mastered them. This part of our organizations is pragmatic. No emotion. Just clear and well-defined parameters we fully understand. Best of all, the numbers and processes ask only for our head work, without the inherent heart work that entangles us when people are part of the mix. Numbers and processes ask much less from us than what we perceive *people* require. We try to be supportive, but it is easy to assume human resources will deal with the bulk of all that *soft stuff*. This perspective is no longer good enough to solve the problems we face today or to meet the challenges ahead in the marketplace, workplace, or community—and our troubled world.

In 2000, futurist, filmmaker, and author Joel Barker shared what he termed a "surprising discovery" as he searched to find the connection between wealth and innovation. I worked with him collaboratively on his groundbreaking film, *Wealth, Innovation and Diversity*. In it, he presents a compelling business case that *"societies and organizations that most creatively incorporate diversity will reap the rewards of innovation, growth, wealth, and progress."* Having a diversity initiative is important, and great organizations have them in place today, but the integrated approach Joel Barker's discoveries suggest—with direct links to innovation and growth—reaches way beyond the best in traditional diversity and inclusion initiatives and programs. His findings note measurable benefits, including producing new kinds of wealth, like the wealth of sustainability, reduced risk, predictability, and innovation in addition to economic wealth.

In 2001, shortly after the launch of his film, we wrote an article together for the American Society of Training & Development (ASTD) called "Leveraging Diversity: Putting Our Differences to Work." In it we offer compelling ideas from our collaborative work about the ongoing struggle both people and organizations have when it comes to sameness and difference, noting seven telling signs that will give you a pretty good indication of what your organization values, not in words but in practice.

SAMENESS OR DIFFERENCE?

Why do we wrestle with sameness and difference as people and as organizations, especially when we have so much to gain by working together? Scientist and author George Ainsworth-Land offered a powerful explanation in his book *Grow or Die*. It is his contention that all things grow and develop within the same three-stage pattern.

For example, we start out focused on our own survival, seeking love, food, and security. In our second stage of growth, starting at adolescence, we begin finding others like us. There are many advantages here. We are validated by others like us. We can accomplish things better together. Since we all talk alike and think alike, decisions and communications are easier.

All of these similarities also increase the level of predictability within our group. We learn to like it. We see equivalent patterns of replication in many of today's organizations for the very same reasons.

So the struggle between sameness and difference is universal. It is part of the evolution of individual and organizational growth—and it is clear as we move further into the twenty-first century, it is time for us as individuals and as organizations to reach for an additional stage of growth. George Ainsworth-Land calls this third stage of growth *mutualism*. In this stage, we come together in different combinations to open the way for innovations leading to new technology, new music, new art, new businesses, new friendships, new cultures, and new opportunities to grow. All of us—east and west, north and south—have to choose between two pathways, and this choice has to be made at every level and in every organization. One way leads us back where *sameness* is rewarded and *differences* are demonized. The other path is toward organizations and communities where diversity, variety, and difference are prized. Why is this so important to our future? Because the people most likely to bring us the paradigm-shifting innovations we need to create new wealth are almost always *outsiders*, people who know little or nothing about the normal way of doing things—people different from us. This is true at every level of every enterprise, community, and country. New wealth is the result of innovation. And innovation is driven by diversity. Diversity is the key that will open the door to the new wealth of the twenty-first century.

Sameness or Difference: What Does Your Organization Value?

Here are seven telling signs:

- ▶ Your leadership team at all levels (including the board) lacks diversity.

- ▶ Old notions, perceptions, preferences, and prejudices still exist; they are sometimes subtle and left unchallenged.

- ▶ Every group or team has its own agenda; efforts are fragmented and lack new ideas from "outsiders" or collaboration for best execution of plans and results.

- ▶ People who are different are rarely hired, developed, promoted, or included; slow progress against stated goals is an indicator.

- ▶ New ideas and innovative thinking are subtly shunned with cynicism, risk aversion, and exclusion or seen as a nuisance—or ignored completely.

▶ The words say you value diversity and inclusion, but your actions speak louder.

▶ You dismiss diversity and inclusion as a human resource issue instead of recognizing that they are drivers of innovation and new wealth; your business plans reflect this view.

Part of our struggle is our search for the words to have meaning. I'm often asked what it means to put our differences to work. It's easy to rattle off an answer like this when someone insists: "Putting our differences to work means creating an environment where people, naturally unique and different—diverse by nature and experience—can work more effectively in ways that drive new levels of creativity, innovation, problem solving, leadership, and performance in the marketplaces, workplaces, and communities of the world." What's always missing in such a definition is how limiting the words are, how ambiguous they are depending on your own differences and experience, and how absent the human element seems to be.

Definitions have their place, but they're only words until we breathe life into them by our actions and example. Let me paint a more vivid picture. Putting our differences to work at every level within an organization requires a new kind of intention from everybody. It means consciously recognizing one undeniable fact: that people are the number one source of new thinking and new ideas needed for change and the betterment of business and society. Here I'm not suggesting that leaders use the phrase as a rhetorical slogan. Remember "People are our greatest asset"? It lost its magic and meaning when the words and actions didn't align. Now it sits on the shelf with other overused phrases. Leading this charge requires a strong belief in people that is reflected day to day in our work and behavior. It calls for us to creatively utilize the many dimensions of diversity within our organizations, in business, and in society to their full potential.

As we've stripped to "lean and mean" and buzzwords like *human capital* and *talent management* have come into fashion, the rippling influence appears to have distanced many leaders from the very heart and soul of achievement in their organizations: the people. It is the heartbeat, commitment, and hard work of every individual that fulfills a business strategy and brings about innovation, leadership, and high performance for any organization or endeavor. Those leaders who consciously and intentionally focus on the mastery of leading the workplace and building diverse teams will be well on their way to pioneering a new era leadership excellence the fastest way.

Numerous studies have followed Joel Barker's pioneering discoveries and my own early study and practice, both affirming our findings and also throwing new questions into the mix. This new thinking calls us to step further inside this compelling issue to get a deeper understanding of where we are today and where we need to go.

One significant study that has created a buzz of controversy is the work of Robert D. Putnam, a distinguished political scientist and professor at Harvard University—and, I must add, a champion for the power that people hold when they work together. You need not wonder where his heart is on this topic if you visit the Better Together initiative (www.bettertogether. org), which grew out of his notable work on civic engagement. The website tagline reflects his call to action: "Connect with others. Build trust. Get involved."

Controversy arose when Putnam's findings were published in "Diversity and Community in the Twenty-first Century" in the *Nordic Political Science Association Journal* in June 2007 and hit the media in sound-byte form. In reading the study, cover to cover, and listening directly to Putnam's personal reflections on it, you realize one of the contributions he made in publishing the study was helping all of us see our own *truth*. We don't trust one another as much as we should, and, consequently, we tend to isolate ourselves, staying with those most like us. Putnam did make these conclusions about his findings in the United States: "It's not merely a fact that America is diverse, it's a benefit. America will—all of us will—benefit from being a more diverse, more heterogeneous place. Places that are diverse have higher rates of growth on average.... In the long term, waves of immigration like we are experiencing are good for society."

What came out loud and clear are honest questions we need to ask ourselves in all segments of society: How have our own behavior and actions, as members of society and leaders in organizations and communities, contributed to such distrust of one another? And what are we going to do about it? How can we rebuild trust by getting to know one another better—and putting our unique talents to work? Putnam suggests that it is having shared values or shared identity that draws us together. There is the reference point from which we have to work.

THE GOOD NEWS ABOUT THE BREAKTHROUGH IN THINKING

The need for a shift in building capability for putting our differences to work has been recognized in an increasing number of recent studies and writings. I began pioneering this new level of thinking in my own work in the early 1990s, documenting it in my Diversity Breakthrough! series in

2000, along with others blazing the trail, like Joel Barker and his work on wealth and innovation, Roosevelt Thomas and his new direction, Taylor Cox, Michalle Mor Barak, and others. However, like all new ideas, it takes time for acceptance to begin to take root, and it has, step by step. Ironically, this *acceptance* happened because of the diversity of studies and books on the subject and a wildly changing marketplace, workplace, and community—you might say it was all of us virtually putting our differences to work that began to build awareness, momentum, and acceptance.

In 2003, for example, the need for new critical leadership skills was affirmed in the five factors of leadership showcased in a book built from the results of an extraordinary two-year study by Accenture, *Global Leadership: The Next Generation*, authored by thought leaders Marshall Goldsmith, Cathy L. Greenberg, Alastair Robertson, and Maya Hu-Chan. Accenture's study validates that knowledge and know-how will be the primary sources of value in the twenty-first century. This means by putting our differences to work, we can multiply the value. The study also contends that the ability to lead people whose backgrounds and values may be radically different from ours requires new skills for leaders at this time in history, including thinking globally, appreciating cultural diversity, developing technological savvy, building partnerships and alliances, and sharing leadership. This isn't enough in itself. In the summary, the study's authors suggest:

> No one leader can be good at everything, which leads us to the conclusion that shared leadership across a team of leaders will be the way in which excellent global companies do business in the future.... Future leaders must know their particular strengths and how to draw upon the complementary strengths of others—sharing leadership roles as needed.

This, too, is a big step forward, but in a distributed workplace in the global marketplaces and workplaces across the world, we need leaders at every level with skills and behavior that are adaptable, putting differences to work wherever we find ourselves.

The good news about building capability for putting our differences to work is that it doesn't require all new skills. To the contrary, it has much more to do with applying what we already know to this challenge, refocusing our attention and reshaping our habits.

I discovered this truth from Peter Drucker, known as the father of modern management. It came to light when I was writing my first book, *Breakthrough! Everything You Need to Start a Solution Revolution*. In his book *Post Capitalist Society*, Drucker points out that most of us tend to classify what we know into specialized areas of knowledge, instead of applying the strengths of all our knowledge to different problems—looking at the problems we face and asking, "What do I know? What have I learned that I might apply to this task?" In a way, this says that we want to put the differences in all our areas of knowledge to work to solve problems. Drucker's wisdom has been a central part of my ongoing work in helping individuals, teams, and organizations around the world put differences to work to create diverse, inclusive environments ever since. I have witnessed over and over again that what it takes to draw differences together is mainly utilizing what we already know about leading change, calling upon the strengths of our experience, *with a little different twist.*

KEY POINTS: PUTTING OUR DIFFERENCES TO WORK

▶ People are the number one source of new thinking and new ideas needed for change and the betterment of business and society. Putting our differences to work means learning to work more effectively in ways that accelerate our capacity to innovate, influence, and bring value to the marketplace, workplace, and society. It is our intention and behavior that breathe life into the words and give them meaning.

▶ It's time for individuals and organizations to reach for a new stage of growth, where we come together in novel and different combinations to open the way for innovations leading to new technology, new music and art, new businesses, new friendships, new cultures, and new opportunities to grow. Diversity has measurable benefits; it produces new kinds of wealth—the wealth of sustainability, reduced risk, predictability, innovation, and economic wealth. (Joel A. Barker)

▶ Currently, we don't trust one another as much as we should; because of this, we tend to isolate ourselves, staying with those most like us. However, diversity benefits society. We need to connect with others. Rebuild trust. Get involved. (Robert D. Putnam)

▶ Future leaders must know their particular strengths and how to draw upon the complementary strengths of others. (*The Global Leader*, Accenture study)

▶ Everybody in a distributed workplace in the marketplaces and communities of the world is a leader; we all need to be prepared. Every day each of us has the opportunity to influence someone or something.

WHO SAYS PUTTING OUR DIFFERENCES TO WORK IS THE FASTEST WAY TO INNOVATION?

To answer this question demands more than an explanation, data, or conclusions from studies. Talk and theory don't meet that standard of proof of what we are capable of doing today. So I searched to find work-in-progress stories that had meaningful concrete results. I hoped to find examples that would also clearly demonstrate that putting our differences to work is in fact the fastest way to innovation, leadership, and high performance. There isn't a shortage of illustrative stories. This book alone has over twenty with great lessons, best practices, and inspiration from which to draw. Finding the right ones as convincing evidence of what putting our differences to work can produce, however, took time, and I set the bar high.

What I wanted most was to identify a couple of pioneering efforts that would set the stage for our discussion in this book, linking leadership and diversity directly to innovation across industries, communities, and the world. There were considerations of inclusion, too. At best, the illustrative cases needed to be broad enough that you and other leaders would find them relevant to your work with issues of common interest to us all. I identified two that create a panoramic view of what we can do together, establishing a new reference point for us all.

The first story, "The Habitat JAM," is one that I personally experienced and in whose rippling influences I continue to be involved. The second story, "Global Innovation Outlook," is one that I didn't discover until I was in the final stages of writing this book. It popped out of nowhere one day when I wasn't even looking. Both stories started with visionary leaders braving new territory. The common ground they share is that diversity and dialogue were key components. Between the two poignant global examples, as you will see, everyone is included in some way.

THE HABITAT JAM

Some doubt that putting differences to work could possibly be the fastest way to get to innovation, leadership, and high performance. At one time, I might have sided with them. Results of the many studies call such an idea into question, including some of Putnam's findings previously mentioned. After all, look around and you don't need a study to show we have our problems getting along and working together. However, when there is bold, visionary leadership, things can be different.

Great *firsts* in history start with an idea and belief in the unseen. Sometimes new possibilities are observed. Sometimes they go unnoticed. Always they cross a threshold, opening the way for more innovation to follow. What I know for sure is that people have the capacity to work together. They can move with speed, dream big, and achieve way beyond what most of us expect. How can I make such a claim? I witnessed it. I was part of it. History recorded it.

On December 1, 2005, nearly forty thousand people logged on to participate in the Habitat JAM, a seventy-two-hour global experiment, when the people of the world came together in an unprecedented online dialogue for the *first time*.

The idea behind the jam was to engage people from all walks of life, including architects, business leaders, planners, teachers, activists, NGOs, bankers, government leaders, slum dwellers, ministers, experts, thought leaders, doctors, entrepreneurs, and visionaries young and old, poor and wealthy all over the world. The goal was to get us working on the most pressing problems of our day for cities around the world. Seven unique forums framed the most critical issues:

> ▶ Improving the Lives of People Living in Slums (two forums)
>
> ▶ Sustainable Access to Water
>
> ▶ Environmental Sustainability
>
> ▶ Finance and Governance
>
> ▶ Safety and Security
>
> ▶ Humanity: The Future of Our Cities

An invitation to participate was open to anyone with something to say about the cities in which they live. The intent was to give people an equal voice to share their thoughts on issues affecting their lives. The plan was to give the people of the world—not the experts—the opportunity to set the agenda for the World Urban Forum III hosted by the Government of Canada in June 2006. Everyone's ideas were gathered, sorted, and refined with a quite miraculous outcome.

The Habitat JAM was a courageous experiment sponsored by the Government of Canada in partnership with UN HABITAT (United Nations Human Settlements Programme) and IBM. The experiment was innovation at its best. It put differences to work for the common good. We talked with

---

Habitat JAM
Who Showed Up?

Architects, business leaders, planners, teachers, activists, NGOs, bankers, government leaders, slum dwellers, ministers, experts, thought leaders, doctors, entrepreneurs, and visionaries young and old, poor and wealthy, all over the world.

Source:
Habitat JAM Summary Report.

each other. We shared and explored ideas. We began putting talk into action.

Together, we etched an indelible mark on history during those unforgettable days, where visionary leadership, technology, and people around the world crossed a new threshold of communication and connection with one another, pioneering a new level of collective problem solving on issues critical to the sustainability of our cities and our planet.

It was serendipitous that our organization got involved. In 2004, I founded the Global Dialogue Center, the newest entity of our Leadership Solutions Companies. It is an online virtual gathering place for people throughout the world (www.globaldialoguecenter.com). It has an intentional focus on leadership, professional, and personal development with the belief that by thinking, questioning, and exploring new ideas together, we can be a catalyst for creating a better world than we know today.

So when I received an email from London from someone I didn't know, introducing the upcoming Habitat JAM, it caught my attention. The vision, possibilities, and the empowering example of leadership ignited a kind of enthusiasm we couldn't deny. It made our whole team want to be part of history in the making. Members of our community found big and small ways to get involved. We did lots of blogging and promotion to spread the word. Eight distinguished thought leaders from our Global Dialogue Center community served as "subject-expert jammers" during the event for the Humanity: The Future of Our Cities forum. No one with a pioneering spirit turned down the invitation.

In a podcast recorded and published before the event, Charles Kelly, Commissioner General of the World Urban Forum III (WUF), the visionary leader who saw the opportunity and went after it, described how the Habitat JAM happened:

The Habitat JAM

December 1–3, 2005

We talked with each other.

We shared and explored ideas.

We began putting talk into action.

We etched an indelible mark on history.

CHARLES KELLY

I discovered the concept of *jamming* reading a *Harvard Business Review* article, talking about IBM's experience with their ValuesJam that engaged 300,000 of their employees in 160 countries. What impressed me was the focus on ideas to action. That is in essence what the World Urban Forum is about. This will be the first time that citizens of the world will have the opportunity, without the filters of national governments or repression, to state their points of view.

In that same podcast, Charles Kelly extended the invitation to participate, one I couldn't overlook. He likened what was soon to take place to being present at some important moment in history, such as October 4, 1957, when the Soviet Union successfully launched *Sputnik I*. NASA cites that, the successful ninety-eight-minute orbit around the Earth, as an event that ushered in new political, military, technological, and scientific developments. I wasn't there in 1957, but how many times in one's life are you invited to be present when some threshold of innovation is being crossed? It was a must.

Also in the same podcast, Mike Wing, Vice President of Strategic Communications for IBM added the perspective of a pioneering spirit, telling about what was to be:

MIKE WING

Jamming is genuinely revolutionary. It is a kind of dialogue, a kind of interaction, a kind of idea discovery and opportunity that simply has never been possible before on Planet Earth. Our experience with jams at IBM has been overwhelmingly positive. It is a trust-based and trust-generating medium. It empowers people in ways that previous forms of organizational communication simply haven't done.... We don't know what is going to happen in Habitat JAM. It is an experiment. It is a fascinating one and one we are very hopeful about.

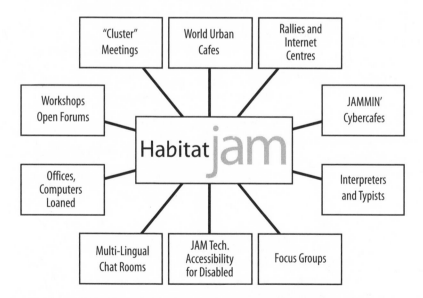

Habitat JAM—Coming Together: Breaking Down the Barriers.
If you had an idea, there was a way to share it. Everyone's ideas and points of view were added to the Habitat JAM database during the jam.

At 17:00 P.M. Greenwich Mean Time, the official clock on the Habitat JAM website began its job—tracking the seventy-two hours we had to participate in the world's largest Internet dialogue on sustainability (see the illustration on the previous page). The world showed up with participants from 158 countries.

Although Habitat JAM was my first jamming experience of this size, I've learned since that there was something very special about this one. It wasn't just the opportunity or the technology or the people showing up that made this jamming experience stand out. There was a distinctive human care and consideration in every detail of how people were included; in how the event was produced; in the way it generated involvement and action around the world; in the way it was directed, facilitated, communicated, and documented.

Not one aspect of the whole event was ordinary. It was extraordinary. Gayle Moss, director of international marketing for Habitat JAM, and her team of committed people-focused innovators created an experience for everyone involved before, during, and after the event that honored the many dimensions of diversity.

Gayle Moss reflected on the experience in a commemorative cover story, "Connecting the World," in *Backbone* magazine (November–December 2006).

GAYLE MOSS

Of the over 39,000 people who participated, many had never touched a computer, but through facilitation and interpretation their voices were heard. We had three makeshift Internet cafés in slums in Africa where facilitators would type on participants' behalf. People were so passionate about getting their voices heard, they found ways to get it done.

Dr. Anna Tibaijuka, an Under-Secretary-General of the United Nations and Executive Director of the UN Human Settlements Programme (UN HABITAT), one of the visionary leaders for the Habitat JAM, shared her personal perspective about what she witnessed and experienced during the event:

ANNA TIBAIJUKA

Kenya had the second-highest number of registrants participating in the Habitat JAM. The fact that thousands have been willing to patiently wait in line, sometimes for hours, in order to be able to contribute to this debate has been a profoundly moving experience for me. The fact that the debate on slums has moved from the academic world to streets and cities such as Nairobi, Dakar, Cape Town and Mumbai, Rio, Lima, and Manila is in and of itself a powerful signal to world leaders on the need for concerted action.

Habitat JAM Results Achieved

The Habitat JAM was an outstanding success in terms of its inclusiveness and global reach. What is even more remarkable is the number of actionable ideas that came from it. More than four thousand pages of discussion and ideas were captured; six hundred ideas generated; and seventy actionable ideas chosen, researched, and summarized in a workbook and CD for the World Urban Forum III, an international UN HABITAT Event on Urban Sustainability held in Vancouver, Canada, in June 2006 with fourteen thousand people attending from around the world.

Charles Kelly summed up the miracle that took place:

> World Urban Forum III (WUF) was unique, reflecting a rather embryonic process that UN HABITAT, under the leadership of Anna Tibaijuka, Executive Director, initiated to bring civil society into the decision-making and sharing about setting the agenda for UN HABITAT. WUF wasn't a policy conference this time. It was a gathering of practitioners from civil society and the private sector, exploring these questions: What things have worked? What have we learned? What mistakes have we made? How do we do things better?

The Rest of the Habitat JAM Story

The goal of the Habitat JAM from the beginning was "ideas to action." The seventy actionable ideas chosen for the World Urban Forum III didn't stop there. One example is the Global Urban Sustainability Solutions Network (GUSSE; www.gusse.org), an online network designed to connect municipal government, NGOs, urban professionals, researchers, business, and citizens —a place where the world is invited to collectively discuss, review, and apply the best ideas for sustainable cities. Many of the ideas were not grand programs with huge budgets. Some were just simple, down-to-earth suggestions that emerged out of necessity to bring unlikely partners together.

I know the spirit of the Habitat JAM still lives. I led a forum called "Being a Good Neighbor." I wanted to talk with others about what it meant to be "good neighbors" to one another. I did. Together, we built a list of attributes, explored creating a charter for cities, and shared ideas on how to keep momentum alive. Bill Tipton, project manager for Hewlett Packard (HP) and contributing author at the Global Dialogue Center, wrote me during the jam expressing what it meant to him to find the Habitat JAM accessible as a blind person: "This is so exciting it makes my hair stand up on end to see and talk with all people with disabilities online."

The Good Neighbors dialogue made the top ten themes in the Humanity forum (see the illustration on the next page). A small group formed to

Habitat jam

1. Education
2. Youth Impact
3. Planning
4. Grassroots Women
5. **Good Neighbors**
6. Children
7. Housing
8. Role of Government
9. Woman's Issues
10. Getting Youth Involved

Habitat JAM—
Top Ten Themes

turn talk into action. Two years later, many Good Neighbor actions have been taken. We meet about every other month for two hours via Skype from the United States and Canada. Early on, we made a decision that the best way we could promote the idea of "being a Good Neighbor" was to use our unique differences in our own spans of influence and support one another in whatever endeavors we chose.

Each of us took a different direction: Carol Roberts accepted an assignment with the U.S. Trade and Development Agency in Kenya related to information communication technology infrastructure. Bill Tipton accepted a leadership role for HP's people with disabilities employee network group. Under his leadership, they've "gone global," connecting HP people across the world. Eric Hellman championed a dialogue at the World Urban Forum III on spirituality's role in sustainability, and he continues to lead dialogues in his community. Avril Orloff turned her artistic talent to graphic illustration to enhance meaningful dialogues for community and business organizations. And me? One contribution was to create a commemorative visual learning exhibit at the Global Dialogue Center's Knowledge Gallery, "We Came to the Habitat JAM: Celebrating Three Remarkable Days in History," to share the experience with people around the world. Come visit at:

www.globaldialoguecenter.com/
habitatjam

The second story, the Global Innovation Outlook, provides a compelling glimpse into the results of a diverse group of cross-industry thought leaders putting differences to work. It again proves people are the fastest way to innovation, leadership, and high performance.

Putting Our Differences to Work
Insights from the Good Neighbor Group Inspired by the Habitat JAM

It's important to value and honor others as a way of valuing and honoring yourself.
—Carole Roberts, United States

Despite our differences, we discovered we care about many of the same things.
—Eric Hellman, Canada

You need to create a caring, open environment for others to share unique ideas.
—Bill Tipton, United States

When hearts and minds are open, we find friends and allies everywhere!
—Avril Orloff, Canada

GLOBAL INNOVATION OUTLOOK

Imagine the power of 248 thought leaders coming together on four continents to talk with one another—a group representing 178 organizations from nearly three dozen countries and regions, in sectors as diverse as aerospace, agriculture, chemical, consumer packaged goods, education, electronics engineering, energy and utilities, environmental services, finance, food and produce, health care, industrial manufacturing, information technology, insurance, logistics, mining, shipping, sporting goods and apparel, telecommunications, and more. This phenomenon occurred at the second gathering in the fall of 2005 of IBM's Global Innovation Outlook (GIO), which hosted a worldwide conversation about the changing nature of innovation.

Global Innovation Outlook—Fall 2005
Who Participated?

1. Academics and university leaders
2. Business partners and clients
3. Government and public sector officials
4. Independent experts and thought leaders
5. Industry analysts and consultants
6. NGOs and citizen interest groups
7. Venture capitalist community
8. Other thought leaders

Source: IBM GIO 2.0 report.

Participants from over twenty-two industries met in San Francisco, Zurich, São Paulo, New Delhi, and Beijing. Together, in fifteen so-called deep dive sessions, thought leaders from businesses large and small, the public sector, academia, citizens' groups, and the venture capital community explored emerging trends, challenges, and opportunities that affect business and society.

This global dialogue centered on three focus areas: the future of the enterprise, transportation, and the environment. Each discussion brought out far-reaching new ideas. It was clear that new ground was broken on every front. The insights emerged from a broad range of topics: from the power of social networks to innovation as a mindset; from small business in going global or finding a niche of success working locally, to a new generation of leaders being prepared for the distributed and virtual business landscape; from innovative transportation breakthroughs for emerging economies, allowing them to "leapfrog" Western nations, transcending old paradigms with new approaches, to noting that the needs of the environment depend largely on the changing behavior of individuals, business, and society—and this is just a small sampling.

One provocative topic that was up for discussion gives a glimpse into the richness of the conversation. It was a discussion around rethinking the idea of "the enterprise," noting it may be outdated and the time ripe for a different approach. Other participants challenged the ideas of "employer" and "employee" as we know them today. Imagine something more flexible, perhaps a collection of loosely formed collaborators who come together on an "opportunity-by-opportunity" basis. From Latin America a bold new vision emerged. The suggestion was that the future might consist of a billion one-person "enterprises"—people moving freely from project to project as their skills and focus shift. In this brave new approach, the traditional enterprise might change its role to include orchestrating and facilitating individuals or groups. With this kind of provocative new thinking came the realization that such collaborative, contribution-based environments would also need new collaborative standards to foster and support such arrangements.

Besides being an exceptional example to fuel our discussion in this book, I find the Global Innovation Outlook particularly meaningful, because it demonstrates the willingness for a corporation to change its ways of conducting business and to also share this work openly with the rest of us. IBM's Chairman and CEO, Sam Palmisano, admitted that the Global Innovation Outlook "marked new territory for IBM itself." He goes on to share that, like many businesses, IBM had previously always conducted its own inside business forecasting. He described the value of these ongoing global dialogues that explore a wide range of topics in this way:

> We learn from our interactions with one of the world's richest and most diverse business ecosystems, and the members of that ecosystem benefit by coming together to tackle difficult issues and to learn from one another. It's a new approach to problem-solving and it works—because the participants understand that their best ideas will only get better by being part of a larger conversation, where they can be debated, vetted, expanded and improved.

His closing words in the Global Innovation Outlook report echo what is also central to this book: "My hope is that you'll find here provocative ideas about the nature of innovation, business transformation and societal change ideas that you can build on and make your own." (See the Resources and Studies section for more information about the Global Innovation Outlook 2.0 report.)

Abraham Lincoln spoke his wisdom about what achievements like these two examples hold for the future, when he said, "That some achieve great success is proof to all that others can achieve it as well."

WHO SAYS PUTTING OUR DIFFERENCES TO WORK IS THE FASTEST WAY TO INNOVATION?

► Visionary leaders with a strong belief in people recognize people are the number one source of new ideas for innovation; they see opportunities to leverage the talent and seize them.

► Valuing differences is demonstrated by a leader's actions and behavior that create an inclusive environment for accelerating the generation of new ideas, multiplying the creative minds working to innovatively solve problems, and opening the way for breakthrough thinking to be shared openly.

► Free-wheeling open dialogue that values differences maximizes the return on the investment for everyone. It helps organizations and people renew themselves; it builds skills and confidence in solving problems and exploring new ideas.

► People want to have a voice, especially to help solve problems that affect their work and lives. They are willing to figure out ways to participate if they know what they have to say matters and will be heard.

► When leaders are willing and open to trying out new ideas that defy the status quo, it can lead to the discovery of better ways of getting things done.

► When you multiply the differences in an inclusive, welcoming environment, miracles can happen, breakthroughs can be realized, innovation can emerge in the fastest way.

> "A leader must earnestly pursue the question,
> *How can I improve my human qualities?*"
>
> —Kazuo Inamori
> Founder and chairman emeritus,
> Kyocera Corporation, Japan

CHAPTER 2

Five Distinctive Qualities of Leadership

Being asked to fundamentally change the rules in how we think, act, and operate as leaders may seem to be a tall order for many of us. At the same time, there is something familiar about being called to change ourselves in order to lead the way. In times of both crisis and opportunity, leaders are often asked to reinvent themselves; to redirect their attention in some significant way in order for them to champion a transformation of some kind. This is one of those times we're being called on to put our differences to work to forge a new path.

As I admit it, my mind again recalls another poignant time in history in my own leadership life when I was reminded that it is the role of leadership to pioneer new trails so others will feel safe to follow. The story may remind you of events in your own life and work.

In many respects, it was a time that seemed a lot like today's environment. There was great upheaval and change in the world, a time clearly marked by the need for change and unprecedented new demands on leaders. Everything around us was outdated. Old notions of command and control no longer worked to our advantage and needed to be refocused. Much like this time, our thinking needed to be shifted in order to begin a new phase of growth:

THE CALL

I found myself sitting with twenty or thirty other men and women in a conference room. Each of us had been called together—flown in from different locations—for what was to be an important assignment. It had an air of *Mission: Impossible*. There was crisis at IBM with a lot at stake, involving people's lives and well-being—people we knew—our customers, our friends, and our families. None of us in the room knew the others that had been invited to this meeting or specifically why we were chosen to be there or what would be asked of us. I remember clearly that the room had a tense feel of uncertainty. With a start, an executive entered the room. He had a piercing gaze as he seemed to look into each of our faces before he said a word. I'm not sure what his impact was on others, but when he spoke, I've forever remembered what he said, looking directly at me, delivering his message. "You have been invited here—at this time in our history—because of all you've enjoyed." A lot flew through my mind in that instant. He was right. I had enjoyed a great deal. Dreams I had never thought possible at one time had come true for me as a woman and as a leader. My work was interesting, with challenge and opportunity. Most of all, it offered great promise for more to learn, more to become—and if I was reading the message right, I had been called here to somehow give back. Soon we discovered that our mission was to help the company take its first steps in making a course correction that ultimately led to IBM's transformation that began back in the 1990s. It was a moment that each of us was being called on to step up to be on the front line of change. It called for us to be adaptable and willing to change our thinking and actions to serve as pioneers of a new era. It was clear that we would be contributing to something far bigger and more far-reaching than any of us could do alone or even collectively, but we would join other leaders, putting our differences to work across the country and the world to help find the new paths of the future.

The need for change is calling us in a similar way. We are the ones—the leaders, the innovators, the aspiring leaders, and individual contributors. We are all being invited to bring all we already know and strengthen our portfolio of skills with Five Distinctive Qualities of Leadership needed for putting our differences to work.

These five qualities aren't the next iteration of leadership tenets. Instead, they invite you to put a "laser-beam" focus on how you think, operate, and behave—considering that every word you speak, every thought you express, every attitude you reveal has a powerful influence on achieving results.

The Five Distinctive Qualities of Leadership also in themselves are "stretching lessons" for us all. They will tug at your consciousness from a number of vantage points. They will mean casting off some bad habits you've perhaps been overlooking—maybe creating some new habits you've needed for a while. Stepping into these leadership practices relies on the truth in that old adage "Practice makes permanent." Are you up to the challenge?

Let's look closely at what it asks of us to put our differences to work and what distinguishes this new level of thinking and action, as well as key behaviors that express them. You'll see that each quality complements the knowledge you already have in our own leadership "toolbox," while guiding you to explore shifts in thinking and behavior. These changes will strengthen your influence, enhance how you connect with people different from you, transform how you lead, and work as a catalyst to achieve higher levels of achievement across your organization.

FIVE DISTINCTIVE QUALITIES OF LEADERSHIP NEEDED FOR PUTTING OUR DIFFERENCES TO WORK

Each one of the leadership qualities described here is intentionally defined using simple words, so they are easy to remember. Each definition redefines the meaning behind these common words for a new time and the new realities in business and society. As you consider each of them, think about how you might change or adapt them to serve the unique needs of your organization and leadership style.

1. Makes diversity an organizational priority. This quality flips everything we have been conditioned to believe. You know, *let's put our differences aside, we are more alike than we are unalike; look at all we have in common.* These remain valuable truths, but when we stop there, our differences are made secondary, sometimes brushed away as if they don't matter. The bigger oversight is that they aren't even recognized as an advantageous stockpile of kindling to ignite for new ideas, breakthrough thinking—the drivers of creativity, innovation, and invention at any level, in any organization or community. Putting our differences to work requires us to do much more than celebrate differences; or merely saying we appreciate them or tolerate them. It means consciously elevating the importance of our diversity and creating an environment that makes it a catalyst for success. Instead, we need to look for differences, welcome them, and utilize them for the good of all, consciously making our differences a priority—part of the mix—for any mainstream practices like problem solving, team building, and decision making. Albert Einstein helped us understand why this is important when he said, "You can't solve problems with the same thinking you used to create them."

KEY BEHAVIORS

▶ Recognize that differences generate new ideas and breakthrough thinking.

▶ Make difference a mainstream business priority in problem solving, team building, decision making, talent management, and overall business operations.

▶ Create a culture of inclusion for innovators at all levels to thrive, recognizing that it is inclusion that accelerates and influences understanding, acceptance, ownership, engagement, collaboration, and the generation of new thinking and new ideas.

2. **Gets to know people and their differences.** This quality expands our thinking, enabling us to see the many dimensions of diversity in a new light. This requires us to respond to the global realities of the twenty-first century by updating, upgrading, and broadening our knowledge, understanding, and appreciation of the many dimensions of diversity. Seeing our differences as organizational assets is new to many of us. More often, anything to do with diversity is deemed a human resources issue or not considered as more than nice to know in mainstream business activities. Putting our differences to work means consciously developing a curiosity, a reservoir of knowledge, and a day-to-day practice that masters how, when, and where to tap into these invaluable resources of unique ethnic origins, cultural perspective, generational insight, global know-how, marketplace understanding, fresh new thinking, challenging new motivations, creative talents, and a wide range of life experiences. In turn, recognizing and appreciating diversity in its broadest sense will help us more effectively work together, learn together, live together, improve our organizations, reach new levels of success, serve customers in more personalized ways, build strong communities, and create breakthroughs in the quality of life for all (see the illustration).

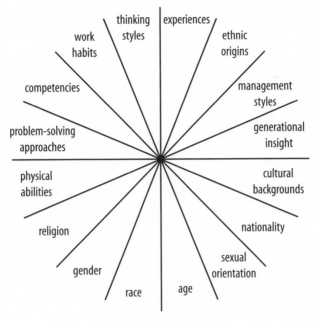

Dimensions of Differences

KEY BEHAVIORS

▶ Develop a curiosity about differences in other people, build a reservoir of knowledge from lessons learned, and establish a day-to-day practice, strengthening these people-focused skills.

▶ Value unique perspectives that come from ethnic origins, cultural backgrounds, generational insight, thinking and problem-solving styles, global know-how, marketplace understanding, and all the dimensions of diversity in people.

3. Enables rich communication.   This quality defies the notion of unilateral streams of thought and closes the gap between layers of hierarchy within organizations of every kind that destroy opportunities for putting our differences to work. It relies on approaching problems with a "beginner's mind"—even as an expert. It reaches beyond asking questions or inviting input, when the past shows little was heard or acted upon. It places a new level of value on what others have to say and ups the ante on responsibility and openness to listen with a new consciousness of mining for the better idea. It dramatically broadens the notion of open, honest two-way communications. How about three-way, four-way, or across-the-world communications? It adds a requirement of trusting ourselves, and each other, enough to engage in action-directed dialogue, across disciplines—welcoming outsiders—in new and different forms that accelerate change and boost productivity in solving problems.

KEY BEHAVIORS

▶ Place a new level of value on what others have to say, always listening for better ideas, a more effective way to lead, and a catalyst for new levels of achievement through others.

▶ Work to broaden traditional ideas of open, honest two-way communication; expanding possibilities like three-way, four-way, or across-the-world collaborations and networks.

▶ Make technology a key tool for enriching communication; invest in developing knowledge and know-how to personally participate and support its use by example.

---

4. Holds personal responsibility as a core value. This quality acknowledges the shift from "institutional loyalty" of the past to the reality of being "free agents" or perhaps other more fluid, mobile kinds of arrangements we've not yet imagined in the marketplaces, workplaces, and communities that are in a continual state of churn. What is added to our way of operating as individuals is the essential quality that Nelson Mandela affirmed: "With freedom comes responsibility." It is a sense of *personal responsibility* that needs to be part of our portable portfolio that goes with us when we move from one job to another at a new company or within an organization, out into the community, or into some new region of the world. Putting our differences to work is greatly enhanced when personal responsibility is a common thread woven tightly into everyone's fabric. This doesn't happen automatically. We have to consciously *install* a sense of personal responsibility into our mindset, so that we are ready for action wherever we find ourselves with an opportunity to influence a positive outcome of any endeavor. Then we have to work hard to instill the habits of personal responsibility through practice so that they are ever-present in all we do. Then, we have an obligation to support, inspire, and encourage each other's mastery of this skill. This might mean acknowledgment; it might mean calling one another on our behavior in a constructive way.

KEY BEHAVIORS

▶ Consciously incorporate personal responsibility into the leadership mindset; then work to imprint the habit of personal responsibility into decision making and actions.

▶ Support, inspire, and encourage others to take personal responsibility, leading by example and by constructively coaching and acknowledging others' actions.

5. Establishes mutualism as the final arbiter.   This quality builds upon its definition: *a doctrine that mutual dependence is necessary for social well-being.* It is also essential for organizational well-being. So this quality applies this concept to all aspects of work and life, as well as all types of organizations. It creates a new definition of success that has a clear "yardstick" that serves as the final arbiter of all plans, innovations, decisions, products, services, programs, profit making, et cetera: *everyone benefits and no one is harmed.* In other words, it creates win, win, win—I win; you win; we all win. Building the future on a foundation of mutualism changes everything we do. It asks more of us, but the benefits are significant. It demands that we consciously make a routine practice of *first* evaluating our actions, behavior, decisions, thinking, and new ideas with a thoughtful inspection of their implications and benefits to all concerned. It adds a new element of consideration to every business or strategic plan. It brings out the best in us all, reversing the traits Mahatma Gandhi warned were perilous to humanity, so that our behavior and actions reflect the values of mutualism: *Wealth with hard work, knowledge with principle, commerce with morality, science with humanity, pleasure with conscience.*

KEY BEHAVIORS

▶ Use a new "yardstick" for success of plans, innovations, programs, decisions, products, services, and profit making: Everyone benefits; no one is harmed—generating mutualistic results: I win; you win; we all win.

▶ Bring out the best in the organization and everyone associated with it: Wealth with hard work, knowledge with principle, commerce with morality, science with humanity, pleasure with conscience (inspired by Mahatma Gandhi, reversing the traits he believed were the most perilous to humanity).

In summary, there is really nothing particularly complex about putting our differences to work. However, it does call for us to operate and think differently. It has much more to do with being aware, adaptive, and willing to make a shift in consciousness. It asks us to pull together what we already know into an integrated supply of ready-to-use knowledge that we have generally kept compartmentalized for far too long. It asks us to take a more thoughtful look at one another—to consider others in everything we do. It calls for enlisting and developing a rich diversity of skills, along with a willingness to apply them to new and different problems and situations than we might be used to doing.

Finally, the motivation for putting our differences to work is best summed up in one of my favorite stories.

> Some years back, my company had the honor of partnering with Hewlett Packard to produce its first global diversity video. It was an internationally recognized, award-winning film called *The Best Place*. One general manager we interviewed for the film left a lasting impression. We asked him why he had gone to such great lengths to bring differences into his organization and put them to work. He replied,
>
> *"When you have ten engineers sitting around a table—and they are all six feet tall, weigh 250 pounds, have an engineering degree, have been around the company for eighteen years, and you give them a problem to solve—they will solve it the same way every time. If this works, fine! In our case, it wasn't working.*
>
> *...If you want to get something different, you have to do something different."*

A NEW BEGINNING FOR LEADERS

Adding these Five Distinctive Qualities of Leadership to your leadership portfolio will take a conscious effort, time to practice, and a conviction to renew yourself in a kind of on-the-job, holistic overhaul. Most of it will be done less with words and more with conscious action. It creates an opportunity for a leader's new beginning. We only get a few of these in a lifetime. When the opportunity arrives, usually unexpected, it is up to us to be adaptive and willing to step up to lead the way down a new path, rewiring all we have down pat. Perhaps you'll feel a sense of awkwardness at first as you put your own signature on the five qualities that have been introduced, but the more you practice, the more skill you'll develop. Soon it will become second nature. You'll be able to measure your own progress, just by seeing the change in results and how people respond to you as you gain new levels of trust and respect. It is, however, a bit of a quiet victory. No bands play.

Unfortunately, many leaders overlook the chance for renewal and settle into the sameness of their entrenched routines. With our organizations, our communities, and our world buzzing with opportunities for innovation, problem solving, leading in our respective fields of influence, and begging for our best performance, allowing yourself to become closed and stagnant is hardly recommended.

Two friends of mine, Tom and Karen, built a sailboat with dreams of sailing around

> **Five Distinctive Qualities of Leadership**
>
> ❶ Makes diversity an organizational priority
>
> ❷ Gets to know people and their differences
>
> ❸ Enables rich communication
>
> ❹ Holds personal responsibility as a core value
>
> ❺ Establishes mutualism as the final arbiter

the world. It took them nearly eight years to finish the boat, leave their full-time jobs, and take off. After a little over a year sailing, they shipwrecked in Fiji and in minutes lost everything. One night after they returned home, Tom shared a poignant moment about how Karen had had a meltdown, as the realization settled in that there was nothing left of what she had known. His response was moving. "Karen, how many times do people get the chance to take all they've learned and start over?"

Interestingly, there are parallels to this story and how some leaders feel today. All that they have known is changing. They invested a great deal of time and energy becoming leaders and building their "boss capital"—developing a style, their way of doing business; their reputation, perhaps as the cynic in the group that has been applauded; or maybe their ruthlessness that has been left unchecked; or perhaps they consistently got the job done with an expected wake of debris and a toll on others—or maybe it's just a quiet complacency that no one has mentioned. They have their well-known preferences for working with those most like them and are definitely more skilled in driving the bottom line, than they are at bringing out the best in people. Well, that leadership model has "shipwrecked," and it's giving us all a chance to start over—to take what we know and apply it to a whole new emerging, ever-changing environment that needs more than what we offer today.

This unexpected evolution of leadership—or at least, this unnoticed evolution, until recently by some—is not completely new. It is true that both the opportunities and the challenges we face in nearly every direction are vastly different than at any time in history, but the human dimension to leadership remains the same. The best leaders across time seemed to emulate their unique version of five distinctive qualities that put differences to work—including the associated behaviors and actions—all quite naturally. Most often, this happened when they stepped up to some compelling call for leadership that led them to reach for something greater than themselves, as all of us are being asked to do now. For example, it wasn't until Abraham Lincoln lost himself in the importance of ending slavery that his life took on a significance he had never dreamed of. By one account of his renewal, "He literally was reborn; he became a new creature." The *Boston Daily Transcript* reported on October 13, 1858, describing Lincoln's new level of leadership as he was observed in the Lincoln-Douglas presidential debates:

Abraham Lincoln
Lincoln-Douglas Debates
The *Boston Daily Transcript*
October 13, 1858

"Lincoln is a tall, lank man, awkward and, apparently, diffident, but when he spoke he was no longer awkward or ungainly; he was graceful, bold, and commanding. For about forty minutes he spoke with a power we have seldom heard equaled. There was grandeur in his thoughts, comprehensiveness in his arguments, and a blinding force in his conclusions which were perfectly irresistible. ... every eye was fixed upon the speaker, and all gave serious attention."

Regardless of stature and station, we are all standing at the intersection of a different new world. In order to accelerate our pace, reap the benefits, and share the leadership for opening the way, we have to step into these new distinctive human qualities and wear them as a coat of arms for the twenty-first century. It will involve recharging and refreshing all that you know, while incorporating a constant flow of refinements to establish and adapt new habits in the way you think and operate. It will no doubt result in many leaders being seen in a new light. This happens to people as others respond to their care and the meaningful contributions—and witness that their leader is fostering a workplace, a marketplace, and a community that reflect the involvement of all its people.

When I think of leadership renewal, Peter Drucker, the prolific business author, well known as the father of modern management, always comes to mind. He had a straight way of talking that left you feeling the true weight of responsibility one carries as a leader. If he were here to help you take on this higher calling of leadership, he would surely get right to the point, stating clearly what he thought in plain talk, as he always did. He summed up the essence of what needs to be considered as you begin to put the Five Distinctive Qualities of Leadership into practice in a message he left behind:

The leaders who work most effectively, it seems to me, never say "I." And that's not because they have trained themselves not to say "I." They don't think "I." They think "we"; they think "team." They understand their job to be to make the team function. They accept responsibility and don't sidestep it, but "we" gets the credit.... This is what creates trust, what enables you to get the task done.

Surely, he would also remind you of the competencies he felt would be most essential for you to change your leadership habits: listening, communicating, reengineering your mistakes, and subordinating your ego to the task at hand.

HOW TO BEGIN YOUR LEADERSHIP RENEWAL

The way to begin is best illustrated by a story told to me by Frances Hesselbein, chair of the Board of Governors of the Leader to Leader Institute (formerly the Peter F. Drucker Foundation for Non-Profit Management) and recipient of the U.S. Presidential Medal of Freedom. She has been a trusted mentor, teacher, and role model for me as a leader. I also saw her tell this story to a room of 2,800 leaders at HP, where, as with Abraham Lincoln, "every eye was fixed upon her, and all gave serious attention to her message." People still remember it and quote it.

FRANCES HESSELBEIN

I was caught in New York City traffic on the way to the airport for a flight to Switzerland. I was thinking about the seventy-three men and women—the key staff members of an international organization I would be working with the next week. They were coming from their posts all over the world and from many cultures, races, languages and backgrounds. I thought how I could open my session on leadership in a way that would connect with the rich mix of culture, race, and ethnicity.

I looked beside me at a bus that also was stalled in traffic. On the side of the bus was a big advertisement—not the usual one. Just a big white placard with four lines:

To achieve greatness:
Start where you are.
Use what you have.
Do what you can.
—Arthur Ashe

It was providential. I took this message from a distinguished North American sportsman, humanitarian, and author, at the tragic end of his life dying of an AIDS-tainted blood transfusion, to people who deal every day with the most difficult human conditions and circumstances, often with massive needs, limited supplies and too few workers. Arthur Ashe's message connected with the realities of their lives. It made sense in any language and it traveled around the world when we said good-bye.

The answers to "How?" and "What?" often are right there in front of us. It just takes a leader with open eyes to recognize it and a willingness to act. Peter Drucker has a nice way of putting it also:

> "Make your contribution.
> Everything else is a diversion."

Are you ready?

CHAPTER 3

The Basics for Putting Our Differences to Work

Before I begin anything, I like to gather what I need to support my journey, whether it is hike, a trip, or a new work project. Something happens when you pull together all the provisions you'll need. There is a momentum that begins to build; the start begins to feel real. This chapter comes from this practice. It brings together four useful tools that serve as a road map, a compass, a checklist, and a little inspiration as you begin putting the Five Distinctive Qualities of Leadership into practice. Each of these tools is foundational to the work ahead.

THE PUTTING OUR DIFFERENCES TO WORK MODEL: Six Steps That Make It Happen

I admit that I'm not really drawn to business models. Mostly, because it's been rare to see business models, in themselves, ignite the human spirit. Far too many of us at all levels, consultants by the scores, and even great change leaders rely on business models as the main source of "inspiration" to engage people, drive action, and achieve results. Where they seem very effective is if they are simple and serve as a visual "road map" to guide the way. The Putting Our Differences to Work Model was designed with this point in mind (see the illustration).

There was a real call from leaders who felt it was critical to have a clear process and actionable steps for putting differences to work. This book

45

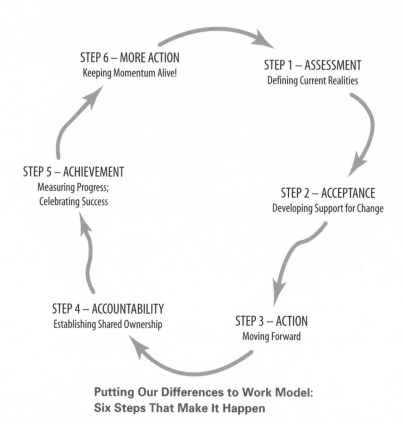

Putting Our Differences to Work Model:
Six Steps That Make It Happen

is built around the action-directed steps of the Putting Our Differences to Work Model. Part 2 includes a dedicated chapter for each phase of change, but in this chapter we will explore the model's basic concepts.

The six-step model depicts the ever-changing, perpetual cycle of *action* that has brought about great change throughout the ages in organizations, institutions, businesses, communities, countries, and the world—and even in individuals. It applies whether you are just beginning a new initiative or direction, taking a next step in an existing one, or revitalizing and refocusing to accelerate results of an effort well underway.

Its *imperfect* circle symbolizes the realities of any kind of change, including the change necessary to make putting differences to work a key driver of your leadership and organizational success. I'm certain you will agree on the basics: What all change has in common is that it requires hard work and resolute determination. It often involves big swings of effort and sacrifice necessary to arrive at the next step. It challenges us to adapt and refine as we go along—and when you reach a moment of success, you soon realize that there remains much more to do to keep the momentum alive. Then, fueled with confidence from our successes, we keep marching on reaching for that next milestone through *more action.*

Each of the model's strategic milestones, applied to a people-focused mission, work to build and renew understanding, involvement, alignment, and ownership required to engage your diverse team of innovators, so that they can move out to reach for new levels of innovation and results at the intersections of all their differences.

As a practice, at its best, the model is a timeless framework that can be applied strategically or even tactically to specific actions. Therefore, you may be working at multiple steps at one time—especially if you are leading or supporting multiple teams, multiple initiatives, or organizations. Each may be at a different milestone requiring different actions. Each may be at a different level of readiness or progress. Personally, with practice, I find it also becomes a mental assessment tool. I'm always looking at situation, project, or any people-focused endeavor asking, "Where are we now?"

CREATING AN ORGANIZATIONAL SNAPSHOT:
Establishing a Reference Point for Change

In the book *Blink: How to Think without Thinking,* Malcolm Gladwell describes the value of the Organizational Snapshot: "the task of making sense of ourselves and our behavior requires that we acknowledge there can be as much value in the blink of an eye as in months of rationale analysis."

Many change initiatives fail. Unfortunately, we tell ourselves this story over and over again, imprinting this limiting belief. One observation I've made over the years is that if a change initiative of any kind fails, there was a flaw in the execution. This is particularly true with "people-focused" initiatives, because we're less skilled at pioneering new ideas in the human dimension of change. We would probably be much further along in mastering our execution of people-focused initiatives if we reviewed what happened in a thorough after-action review when a failure takes place. However, who has time for self-examination of a dead issue? Instead, we commonly just start a new initiative with the same inherent flaws. So how do you avoid this pitfall as you work to master the art of putting differences to work in your organization or community? Simply create a reference point—a quick "snapshot" will do, using what you know and refining later.

Establishing a reference point for putting differences to work is *not* the laborious assessment process that involves task forces, consultants, detailed analysis on charts and graphs that generally go nowhere, and months of meetings that delay getting anything accomplished.

It is actually the first step in pioneering a new paradigm that changes all the rules. You simply take stock of where you are as you would on a map based on your knowledge and gut feel.

Let me share an analogy that will help put it in perspective: Establishing your position is a lot like what you would do if you were beginning a hike to the top of a mountain. Before you hit the trail, you check the weather and conditions on the trail. You look for the sign that shows the miles to your destination. When you have your backpacks loaded up, the gang gathers around that trailhead marker (usually pointing at the miles ahead), and you take a snapshot marking the start of your adventure—and you're off! As you hike, you stop at in-between places to rest for a minute, reassessing your position, seeing if the weather is holding, noting any changes in the trail conditions, and grabbing another snapshot to capture in permanence the progress you've made. You repeat this pattern until you reach the top, where you can see the magnificent view, taking the cherished snapshot at the summit—results achieved!

Whether you are launching a new initiative focused on putting differences to work in your organization or community, or you are integrating its concepts to renew and revitalize an existing effort, the same simple process for creating your organizational snapshot applies.

The Organizational Snapshot illustration shows the worksheet used to create a "snapshot history" of your initiative. This sample depicts that three "organizational snapshots" have been taken over the course of sixteen months, pinpointing the readiness in key areas of organizational influence at specific moments in time. You can see at a glance that *leadership* and *ownership* were the biggest challenges initially. It also shows that the *culture* of

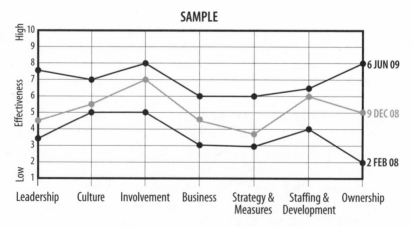

Putting Our Differences to Work Organizational Snapshot

the organization had a higher readiness for change, creating an anchor from which to build in support of putting differences to work. The latest snapshot clearly indicates that progress has been made.

The most valuable part about taking an organizational snapshot, like those shown in the sample, is that it takes *minutes* to create. Each snapshot represents a small investment of time to *think*, with a return on the investment that may prove to be priceless. As each snapshot in time is added, it serves as a leadership quick reference tool that you will want to keep handy, like you would a map and a compass on a big climb.

As a leader, the organizational snapshot tool helps keep you focused on the big picture of your strategic mission at hand, not just the tactics that are in constant churn. It keeps you focused on your ultimate goal of weaving considerations of putting our differences to work into the fabric of the organization and its culture.

Word of Caution

How you use an organizational snapshot, particularly in the early stages of an initiative, is as important as using it at all. It's not intended to "sell" your need for change or to publicly share in a slide show, unless you are claiming some big victory that reflects on how far you've come. My strong recommendation is that you, and perhaps your small core team, use it to build and execute your strategy.

As a leader, I've most often used an organizational snapshot quietly and recommended the same to other leaders with notable success, allowing it to be my own personal "strategy room" at a glance. I carry it with me, either in my head or at my desk or some other safe place. It's never far from my thoughts. Sometimes, I find myself taking a stream of snapshots when it makes sense versus waiting for any given timetable. Leading change is alot like a chess game: every move matters. Often the shifts in the landscape change the picture. So, my "mental camera" is never far away. Rarely are there occasions when I've used a snapshot directly in a slide presentation. Instead, when some big jump in progress shows up, I use it as a prompter to recognize and reward. If it shows a big dip down in progress, it calls for thinking and action to shore up the weak spot without looking to blame or do anything to discourage. Instead, I use it as an opportunity to renew, redirect, and see where focused attention is needed.

How to Take a Snapshot

Look at the categories shown across the bottom of the organizational snapshot in the illustrative sample. They represent key areas of significant

influence on the overall effectiveness of creating a diverse, inclusive environment—one
that is striving to put differences to work.
They are also areas of significant influence
for any kind of change. They represent the
system of considerations needed to renew
and strengthen any organization.

After reviewing the illustrative sample,
follow this step-by-step process to take your
organizational snapshot:

> **Organizational Snapshot**
>
> ❶ Create online and print, or
>
> ❷ Download PDF (8½ × 11).
>
> *Refer to the Resources and Studies section.*

▶ For each area, select a number from 1 to 10 that best represents
  your organization's current level of effectiveness or readiness based
  on your knowledge (1 is low; 10 is high).

▶ On the vertical lines on the snapshot worksheet, plot the level of
  current readiness and/or effectiveness of each area of influence,
  considering how well it is positioned to support putting differences
  to work to drive success. Here are considerations for each area of
  influence:

Leadership
- Involvement
- Sponsorship for *the fastest way* to success through people
- Diversity at all levels; inclusion valued
- Buy-in for putting differences to work
- Five Distinctive Qualities for leaders at all levels
- Leaders' behaviors/actions aligned

Culture
- Value based; people focused
- Supports change
- Five Distinctive Qualities for leaders at all levels
- Diversity and inclusion integrated into fabric; key considerations
  of the culture

Involvement
- Participation at all levels from everyone
- Putting differences to work consciousness

Business
- Readiness for multicultural, global realities, changing marketplace
  and community
- People valued as the drivers of innovation, leadership, and high
  performance

* Putting differences to work as a key business priority
* Support for mutualism as the final arbiter

Strategy and Measures
* Vision
* Strategy
* Tactical plans
* Measures
* Systems
* Compliance with regulations
* Reviews
* Alignment

Staffing and Development
Diverse and Inclusive
* Hires
* Promotions
* Recognition
* Development, including Five Distinctive Qualities for leaders at all levels
* Mentoring
* Training

Ownership
* Standards established for individual contribution and recognition of them
* Incentives built in to drive innovation, effective collaboration, and high performance
* Performance incentives for mastery of Five Distinctive Qualities

In summary, all leaders hold a responsibility to *think*—to be in a constant state of questioning and adjusting direction. Regularly creating organizational snapshots is one leadership tool to help you fulfill this responsibility. It is an invaluable practice for mastering the skill of execution of plans that are second to none.

I admit it. This responsibility was drilled into my consciousness as a young leader. Although he was long gone when I showed up, Thomas J. Watson Sr., founder of IBM Corporation, left a compelling message behind that was passed down to me and other leaders:

All the problems of the world could be settled easily if [we] were only willing to *think*. The trouble is that [we] very often resort to all sorts of devices in order not to think.

Over the years, the organizational snapshot concept—a concept to prompt you to think for yourself—both the formal worksheet and the virtual "embedded-in-your-mind" version, has been refined and adapted to many types of change initiatives, big and small. I encourage you to make it work for you, so it fits your unique organization and leadership style.

 Organizational Snapshot Prompter
Part 2, "Knowledge and Know-how to Guide the Way," includes prompters to remind you to use this tool as you move through each step of change. Look for the camera symbol. Most of all, try it! It truly works.

PRINCIPLES FOR SUCCESS

A set of operating principles works across all six steps of the Putting Our Differences to Work Model to maximize success. These principles can be a powerful "energy source" for leading the way in your organization.

▶ **Mark your starting point.** As noted, part of getting started at any of the six steps is taking an organizational snapshot of where you are, which will establish a reference point. It will help you set your direction, and later, it will make it easy to measure progress and celebrate your successes in putting differences to work. It also helps you spot and track trends over time in a very simple way. As Albert Einstein taught us, "The important thing is not to stop questioning." This principle helps you build an ongoing practice of scanning the environment, reevaluating, adjusting each critical move, while keeping plans fluid, so they move and adapt to the ever-changing realities of an organization.

▶ **Be willing to jump into the middle of what's going on.** There is never a better time to take a bold step forward in putting our differences to work. Nothing stops so you can start. Since the work is integrated into every aspect of your organization, you have to be ready and willing to jump into the middle of all that going on at each critical goal-directed step.

▶ **Be prepared to work a parallel path.** Putting our differences to work requires skills in working two paths at once. One will be visible. One will be quietly working behind the scenes, using clout, influence, knowledge, know-how, and inspiration to open the way for success. Every move counts, so choose them thoughtfully.

As you put these principles into practice, remember that you are pioneering a new paradigm. Some sage advice from the Joel Barker film

Paradigm Pioneers applies: "Rely on your intuition to make good decisions with incomplete information. Have courage to take a risk. Understand that time is needed to move from rough concept to a new working paradigm."

TALKING WITH PEOPLE:
Common Mistakes Leaders Make

All leaders want to be great! Don't you? The organization, and everyone in it, needs you to be great. To complement your new approach in building rich communication, here are three common mistakes leaders make in their desire to connect with people (I first shared these in *Communications World* magazine, September–October 2007).

- ▶ **Leaders often talk *at* people versus *with* them.** Many seem fearful about sounding too personal or human, as if it were a weakness. Instead of saying, "I've been looking forward to talking with you about our company," the leader has a one-way talk about "the company's strategic imperative to *engage* employees," forgetting how it feels to learn that leadership is out to *engage* you.

- ▶ **Leaders say *what they want* without considering *what employees need to hear*.** Those statistics and graphs are impressive, but most employees are longing to find out more about the leader's vision, how they fit into it, how much the leader needs and values their contributions.

- ▶ **Leaders use too much head talk and not enough heart talk.** Buzz words, shop talk, and B-school jargon are shelters to hide behind for many leaders. Using them is safe territory, has no emotional connection, and means little to almost everybody listening.

As a new leader at IBM, I heard a presentation about Winston Churchill, one of the twentieth century's great leadership communicators, given by James Humes, a well-known presidential speech writer and author of *Churchill: Speaker of the Century*. His wisdom has stayed with me and with practice became a reliable yardstick for measuring meaningful messages for myself and other leaders. Churchill's five elements for great oratory are (1) a strong beginning, (2) one theme, (3) simple language, (4) use of analogy, and (5) appeal to the human side of a person. If your message ever misses having the impact you wish it would, one of these elements is missing. You'll be surprised how these work!

MOVING FROM THOUGHTS INTO ACTION

We've come to a decision point—an intersection that tugs at the heart of the leader to make a conscious choice. Do you choose to turn back, remaining the same, ignoring the compelling call at this point in history? Or do you choose to be one of the new breed of leaders, taking all you know together with your vision and pioneering spirit to forge a new path—one where putting our differences to work is the driver and differentiator of business success? You've heard the argument for the need for change. You've been given five distinctive qualities to adopt, adapt, incorporate, and practice to support your mission. You have six steps that serve as a road map, a tool for taking an organizational snapshot to use as a compass, and a set of operating principles to maximize success. The decision is yours. My own decision is fueled by an earlier experience.

One time, having reached a similar intersection, I traced how "dreams had come true" for me in business during the previous twenty years at IBM. My hope was to bolster up my courage to make the right decision to blaze a new trail. The tracing resulted in my writing a simple poem. Flowing from my memory, the reflection filled me with confidence enough to say, "Yes!" to a new calling. The poem has been used by many trailblazers over the years and has since been translated into sixteen languages, which validates that its message is universal. Joel Barker has used it for many years to close his presentations about vision and encouraged me to rename it "*Our Dreams in Action.*"

Interestingly, I discovered recently that when the words of the poem are centered on the page, the lines create an equidistant cross. According to Angeles Arrien, a cultural anthropologist, in her beautiful book *Signs of Life*, the equidistant cross shape—the plus sign—universally symbolizes the process of relationship, integration, and balanced connection. For those hearing the call to innovate, lead, and reach for new levels of peak performance and contribution, the poem also demonstrates once again that putting our differences to work is a powerful practice familiar to us all. May it inspire a "Yes!" in you as you move into action.

OUR DREAMS IN ACTION

Dreams give us hope.

Hope ignites passion.

Passion leads us to envision success.

Visions of success open our minds to recognize opportunities.

Recognition of opportunities inspires far-reaching possibilities.

Far-reaching possibilities help us enlist support from others.

Support from others keeps us focused and committed.

Focus and commitment foster action.

Action results in progress.

Progress leads to achievement.

Achievement inspires dreams.

Dreams give us hope.

by Debbe Kennedy

PART 2

Knowledge and Know-how to Guide the Way

“Know-how is what separates leaders who perform—who deliver results—from those who don't.”

—Ram Charan
Author, *Know-How*, and coauthor, *Execution*

STEP 6 – MORE ACTION
Keeping Momentum Alive!

STEP 1 – ASSESSMENT
Defining Current Realities

STEP 5 – ACHIEVEMENT
Measuring Progress;
Celebrating Success

STEP 2 – ACCEPTANCE
Developing Support for Change

STEP 4 – ACCOUNTABILITY
Establishing Shared Ownership

STEP 3 – ACTION
Moving Forward

Knowledge and know-how play big roles in putting our differences to work. What is profound about this kind of people-focused expertise is that it rarely takes the form of a big initiative. It is driven more by actions than words and hype and new websites. The most influential actions are often seemingly small shifts in behavior. Sometimes they are subtle, even insignificant, changes or commonplace conversations that have sweeping influences in a short time on engaging people—influences that can and will open the way for new levels of individual and organizational achievement. You'll be surprised how you can influence fundamental change by simply removing a roadblock, changing a few attitudes, raising consciousness about conduct, increasing opportunities for conversation, and making people your personal priority in ways that they know it.

One senior leader I worked for once told me he really wasn't into the "people part" of our business and that my job was to make him look like he was interested and cared, while he worried about more important parts of the business. It was definitely a putting-our-differences-to-work experiment, which worked for a while but became transparent to everyone. Managing the business of an organization is only part of a leader's job. Leading people and creating an environment that thrives on their differences means stepping beyond our comfort zones of business expertise. The return is well worth it.

Many of us want answers to those doubting thoughts that linger in our minds before we are willing to take action or even try anything new and different—*Where is it working? How do I do it?* and *Prove it to me first.* In

Part 2, we are going to focus on answering these questions for each phase of change. In addition, let's also consider a more empowering perspective as you get started.

One observation I've made over the years is that we are consistently much more courageous, creative, and full of innovative ideas than this story of doubts or its questions suggest. I've witnessed the crustiest, risk-averse leaders have breakthrough experiences in solving their own problems in a short time, sometimes in a matter of minutes. This happens with just a few stimulating possibilities to fuel our own creative thinking and action. I liken this experience to how a long-jump athlete takes a running start before actually jumping. Ideas create momentum. Someone else's ideas work like springboards to the discovery of your own powerful ideas. All of us have witnessed this happen. A few suggestions to prompt thinking—and *breakthrough!*—a much better idea is born, custom-made for your organization and its people. This again proves no one knows better than you do about what is needed, even when it comes to putting differences to work. You just need the opportunity to reach inside to find your own answers.

In Part 2, Chapters 4 through 9, you have a chance to explore and focus on knowledge and know-how about each phase of change, applied to putting our differences to work. First-person best practices stories, as well as wisdom from other thought leaders, make the knowledge real and relevant to a leader's day-to-day experience. The stories and wisdom shared reach across industries, as well as public, private, and community sectors. This was intentional, because it demonstrates on still another level how much we can learn from one another—from people who at first glance may seem to be "outsiders" to our individual work. In essence, this book itself puts differences to work, including contributions from corporate life; small and medium businesses; from education, health care, church leaders, government, and military; from global citizens and trailblazing pioneers of innovation through people. Some examples show large-scale impact. Some are seemingly small but far-reaching; while others are up-close lessons learned from leaders willing to share experiences that shaped their capability and capacity to effectively put differences to work. At the end of each story, I note its key points to help you see the most important messages. There are strategy and tactical ideas at the end of each chapter to stimulate your own thinking and action, along with a personal call to action as an inspiring send-off.

Come along.... Stimulate your mind with knowledge and know-how about the fastest way to innovation, leadership and high performance—*putting our differences to work.*

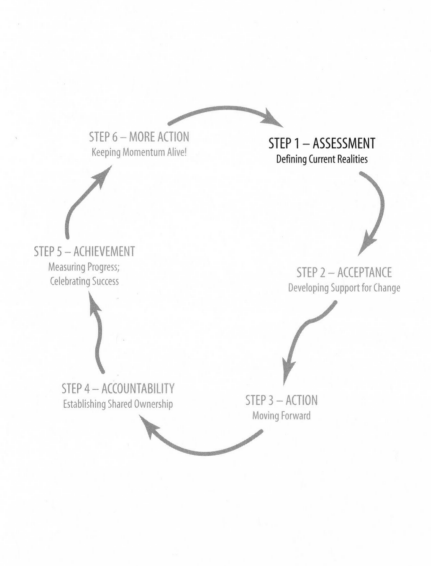

STEP 6 – MORE ACTION
Keeping Momentum Alive!

STEP 1 – ASSESSMENT
Defining Current Realities

STEP 5 – ACHIEVEMENT
Measuring Progress;
Celebrating Success

STEP 2 – ACCEPTANCE
Developing Support for Change

STEP 4 – ACCOUNTABILITY
Establishing Shared Ownership

STEP 3 – ACTION
Moving Forward

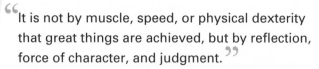

> " It is not by muscle, speed, or physical dexterity that great things are achieved, but by reflection, force of character, and judgment. "

—Marcus Tullius Cicero
Ancient Roman scholar,
orator, and statesman

CHAPTER 4

Step 1—Assessment: Defining Current Realities

It is doubtful any of us would put self-assessment of ourselves or our organizations on a list of our favorite pastimes. However, the process itself is freeing. It feels good to know where we are, how we are, and what challenges lie ahead. It is the unknown that weighs on us. It often keeps us awake at night. It delays our important actions. In turn, it tugs at our self-confidence. If you ignore its call long enough, the unknown can come as an unwelcome surprise—even a shock. What we assumed was going well becomes compromised by inattention. Things often become much more complicated when others take notice first. Simple issues can turn into a crisis—and before we know it, we have *big* problems to solve.

With a focus on putting differences to work in any organization, the role of self-assessment becomes more than a process to keep you and your organization out of trouble. It has a much higher purpose. Building in both formal and informal ways to involve and engage people in the process of ongoing self-assessment as an organization, or as a leader, creates the foundation for change and a continuous cycle of renewal. At the same time, it can be a powerful catalyst that sparks new ideas and innovation. For the best of leaders, self-assessment is never considered an event to be checked off the *to do* list or delegated without personal involvement and interest. It is a regular practice woven into the mainstream of day-to-day business.

This people-focused process takes practice. I assume you have known or experienced firsthand a leader who effectively incorporates self-examination into his or her leadership work as a natural course of business. One leadership example that instantly comes to my mind is Emily Duncan, former Vice President of Culture and Diversity at HP. She left a legacy with an enduring set of accomplishments. Even in her leaving, she used what she often termed "the direct approach." She went directly to the people, honoring their accomplishments and pointing out what it meant to HP to put differences to work across the world. She also used this unique platform to establish a reference point for the work that would follow, clearly placing the baton into the hands of a new generation of leaders. In her farewell letter, she wrote:

> After 22 rewarding years, I wanted to connect with you in a moment of reflection on all we've worked together to accomplish. HP's diversity and inclusion journey bears many fingerprints. We are a recognized leader today and we have a great deal to be proud of as we look back at the distance we have traveled.
>
> When I joined HP in 1985, *diversity* and *inclusion* were new ideas, which we didn't fully understand. Later, we worked together to put meaning behind the words at HP. Then we boldly forged the uncharted path that has resulted in diversity and inclusion being business priorities for the company across the world today.

She received hundreds of messages from across the world. Many people told stories of their own personal achievements; many communicating back that they *got the message* and were ready to move ahead as leaders in their own right.

This direct approach Emily relied on took many forms over the years. In an interview with her one time, she talked openly with me about this powerful practice of ongoing assessment, sharing her perspective on a specific milestone—one we worked on together to reach as collaborative partners:

EMILY DUNCAN

At HP, talking directly with people has always been part of our ongoing renewal process. We've made sure the path has been filled with many opportunities for dialogue as a means of assessing where we were and where we needed to go next. One example that demonstrates the way we have used dialogue as a catalyst for new levels of innovative change is the worldwide conversation we held with over three hundred of HP's senior managers. It was sponsored by a team of senior executives focused on developing and driving diversity initiatives worldwide that we called the Diversity Leadership Council.

There was only one hour available on the agenda at the annual senior leaders' meeting hosted by the CEO. We had specific goals and data we wanted to collect. We found no tested method or process for having such a dialogue in one hour with so many people and such ambitious objectives. However, we put a small team together to figure it out. The format we decided on included twenty-five simultaneous dialogue sessions. There was a multitude of obstacles to overcome. In the end, there was a whole lot of faith put in people. The investment resulted in over three hundred managers learning from one another by sharing their experiences and challenges in creating an inclusive environment that puts differences to work. It also provided us with over two thousand specific insights and creative ideas that helped us build the foundation for what became HP's Diversity Accountability Framework for Managers. Over time, around the world, HP people have found creative ways to tailor the framework to meet their unique needs— a rippling influence of that one-hour conversation.

You can learn a lot about where you are and where you need to go from talking with others. If I want to know what people think— where they stand and what they need in order to contribute more— I ask them. It often opens the way for new possibilities and provides valuable input for strategic decisions—and sometimes it feels real good inside when I see, through others, that all the hard work is making a difference.

Emily's story highlights the power of the direct approach. Talking with people, inviting them into the process of self-assessment, has a number of advantages. First, people like to be included and share their ideas. The fact that they do accelerates their acceptance, understanding, and ownership for whatever emerges afterward, because they were part of it.

As you explore this chapter, you will discover that there is much to learn from other leaders' best practices and lessons learned about the value of the assessment process. You'll see there are different ways to effectively get the job done in any part of your business. We also learn that innovation doesn't always come wrapped in a "paradigm-shifting" idea; or at least one we recognize. Paradigm shifts are often associated with radical change—you know, the kind with a big, dramatic sea change. What we learn from day-to-day leadership practice is that through ongoing renewal that includes regular assessment of current realities, we end up fundamentally changing the existing rules, but incrementally, step by step in a constant forward motion.

Radical change through ongoing renewal is an approach that minimizes the impact of change on people and the organization. It eliminates destruction and unnecessary debris to clean up. And if people are engaged in cocreating the new direction or change in policy or practice, they are more likely to accept what's new and different. The environment remains dynamic, always getting prepared for the next idea.

The importance an ongoing process of self-assessment plays in putting our differences to work (or any other related action, for that matter) is demonstrated in a simple lesson learned early in my life. We lived in a house with fifty-six windows. My mother insisted that at least five windows a week be washed. This always seemed crazy to me. One day, I asked her why this was so important. She told me that by washing a few windows at a time as a regular part of our chores, the windows were always clean, the house was filled with light, and the task of washing them was never a big job.

KEY POINTS: ASSESSMENT

▶ Ongoing assessment keeps you focused.

▶ It helps recognize and celebrate progress.

▶ It helps build confidence and pride.

▶ What you learn becomes your compass.

▶ The process keeps your organization's windows to the future clean and the way clear.

▶ It ensures a constant stream of new light on what needs your attention in order to take the fastest route to innovation, leadership, and high performance through people.

▶ Because it is a routine practice, you won't be overwhelmed with the job.

THE FASTEST WAY IDEAS
FOR STEP 1—ASSESSMENT

Organizational Snapshot Prompter
Before filling your mind with others' ideas, take a quick organizational snapshot. It will give more meaning to the best practices stories, strategy, and tactical ideas that follow (see the Resources and Studies section).

Most of us know exactly what to do in our own organizations, if given time to think about it. With all the pressures of day-to-day leadership, I dare say, we sometimes find ourselves in lonely moments, sitting in front of a blank screen trying to figure out where to begin—usually with a tired mind, overflowing with a day's input. Does this scenario sound familiar? Or, even more commonly, we allow anything and everything to divert our attention. This isn't always intentional, but let's face it—it's easier to do something that we can do without thinking. So we sometimes ignore issues as long as we can. However, let's put our differences to work right here and now and see what emerges for you.

I've selected three stories from different types of organizations. Each demonstrates a unique experience with lessons learned or innovative approaches used by a leader or group of leaders to take this bold assessment step. In each case, you'll find key points to take away, followed by a few strategic and tactical ideas that you can easily tailor to your needs; better yet, perhaps they will serve as a catalyst for you dreaming up just the right creative approach for you and your team or organization. What becomes clear from each story is a point made in the first best practice from education: regardless of our business or organization, big or small, we all have one thing in common—people with the same desires. You will continue to see this truth come to life as the stories unfold throughout the book.

Best Practice—Education

The whole idea of a conference changes when you consider that it is a place where attendees give and receive more than what is listed on the agenda. When it comes to conferences, I've found it particularly gratifying to strip myself of the "networking aspirations" that are pumped up to be essential for any business leader. Instead, I work at attending with a "beginner's mind."

In the beginner's mind there are many possibilities.
In the expert's mind there are few.

—Shunryu Suzuki

I attend with no pockets full of business cards. No personal wants; I just show up to *be* with others. It is also a time for self-assessment and renewal if one is open to it. I've sometimes even picked conferences where I knew the people would represent a broad range of differences. This is how I met Bert Bleke, then Superintendent of Lowell Area Schools in Michigan. I walked in a little late to a banquet at a conference. All the tables with people seated were full and bustling with happy chatter. Bravely, I pulled out a chair to sit at an empty table. I remember feeling awkward at being alone at such a big event. So, I was really glad when Bert walked in with no place to sit, either, introducing himself and joining me.

During the evening, he told a remarkable story of putting our differences to work. It tells about the importance of coming together, starting with the bold step of assessment. It also demonstrates the beginnings of applying the Five Distinctive Qualities of Leadership in the process.

BERT BLEKE

It is interesting how easy it is for most of us to think that our organizations are unique. I've been lucky to have had experiences in education, business, nonprofits, and churches—and I have realized there are many more similarities in the challenges we face than there are differences. The greatest similarity I see—one we tend to forget—is that all our organizations are about people with the same basic needs and desires. The only thing that is truly different is our unique end product. Consequently, we should be able to learn from each other about leading change and making our schools and organizations, businesses, and communities better places for everybody.

For us, change started by people coming together. Three hundred people gathered—students, parents, teachers, administrators, and clergy. In a period of a few hours, we came up with five character traits we felt would be the most powerful influence on kids, our organization, and community: responsibility, integrity, compassion, honesty, and respect. We chose the words based on everyone's input, but we did not define them. Then over a period of the next year or so, we let our schools gradually talk about them and ask themselves, What do these core values mean to us? How can they be important for us? We have worked diligently to instill these character traits not only into our kids but also saying to our employees, our parents, our churches, our community, the process has enabled us to start talking with each other about character and values—it has given us a common language for change.

The character of our students, our organization, and community dovetail with the values of diversity and inclusion. If you think about responsibility, integrity, compassion, honesty, and respect, they make it all fit hand-in-hand together. It is simple. There are signs of change everywhere—but the process is ongoing. Every time I hear, "That wasn't a very compassionate thing to do," or "Gee, that isn't very respectful," I smile. Character is an important part of what kids need for preparation for the real world. It is what we all need.

> **KEY POINTS:** BERT BLEKE'S STORY
>
> ▶ Coming together is a great place to begin defining current realities and experiencing putting differences to work; inclusion accelerates acceptance, understanding, and ownership.
>
> ▶ A diverse group with common interests, but different perspectives, can creatively assess needs and build a framework for change in a short time
>
> ▶ Thinking and questioning helps everyone internalize the change and align their thinking and commitment; ongoing thinking and questioning helps keep us all on track.

Best Practice—Medium-Size Business

Walking into Sue Swenson's office was a distinctive experience. We had met previously, but meeting her on her own turf was a memorable experience. Sue is now President and CEO of Sage Software—North America and has long been a role model of executive leadership, blazing new trails and leading exponential growth in the telecommunications industry for over fifteen years, including as Atrinsic, Amp'd Mobile, and T-Mobile, President and Chief Operating Officer for Cricket Communications, and President and Chief Executive Officer for CellularOne. Wherever she goes there is some entrepreneurial adventure underway.

On my last visit with her, I had come to conduct an interview with an executive, very conscious of the allocation of time scheduled. What I didn't anticipate was that she had blocked the rest of the afternoon and would proudly, and personally, spend it openly sharing and showing me how she went about bringing out the best in people. She told one story of how their leadership team approached this notion of assessment and how she learned more about herself in the process:

SUE SWENSON

I recall an experience some years ago. Our leadership team thought it would be a good idea to bring someone in to help us learn more about our organization—an in-depth look inside. We brought in an external consultant to help us. The idea was that the consultant would assist us in creating a reference point for change by having a series of conversations with people. I selected someone with a no-nonsense approach. The process took about three or four months and was well worth it.

Initially, he helped us find out about ourselves. There were some discovery sessions with each of us on the leadership team. The idea was that before you start finding out about others, it is important to first learn about yourself as a leader. This was an interesting experience for me. I had a chance to explore my own values and learn about the experiences that shaped who I am. I discovered something about myself in the process. I had not recognized my focus on fairness and how important fairness is to me in everything that happens in the business—in terms of equality of opportunity, equality of development, the lack of importance I consciously place on level or status, and my emphasis on making sure everyone is treated fairly. So, where did that come from?

It was an interesting discovery for me to see the early influence. When I was younger, I didn't want to compete in a sport where your success was based on someone's subjective judgment. I wanted to be judged more by substance than form. So I swam. It was about me and the stopwatch. I recognize now that may be why I place so much emphasis on establishing goals that can be compared and benchmarked against similar organizations.... It's about being fair. The person is in a position to control the outcome.

This introspective experience helped all of us understand ourselves and each other better. What I've learned remains important. I want people to be who they are. They don't have to look the same, or be the same, to be successful. It is *substance* over *form* that is valued.

KEY POINTS: SUE SWENSON'S STORY

▶ Putting differences to work more effectively sometimes starts with senior leaders doing some self-assessment themselves to create a reference point for change.

▶ Reexamining values and reflecting on experiences as a leader can help you see your strengths and the differences you bring to the organization and the leadership team.

▶ Introspection with a leadership consultant helps you learn about yourself and others, so that you can make differences key drivers of your success.

Best Practice—Military

It was 1999. When I arrived at the Pentagon, it was one of those spectacular days. Standing outside waiting for me was Jan T. Swicord, then Major, U.S. Army, assigned to the Strategic Human Resource Management Office. She had a striking countenance and stance of an officer with a unique warmth and spirit that made the Pentagon a welcoming place. I had time to visit with Jan before meeting with Lieutenant General David H. Ohle, U.S. Army and Deputy Chief of Staff for Personnel, and his leadership team. She spoke proudly of the work they were doing and openly shared what it had been like to come up the ranks as a woman leader. She also talked about the value of one of the programs instituted for the assessment process:

JAN SWICORD

One of the Army values is respect—respect for others, respect for ideas, respect for different perspectives. Values matter here, and we have learned they need to be talked about and internalized through personal relationships. We also recognized that our traditional approach to instruction in a group of five hundred soldiers—"Let's talk about equal opportunity"—just didn't work.

"Consideration of Others" is one example of our renewed focus and approach to values in the Army. The concept was created at West Point to help the cadets in better understanding each other. Soldiers have the same need, so it was easily adapted. It is designed for the squad leader or small team leader. Once a quarter, leaders have to sit down with subordinates and discuss issues relevant to their job set. It is not one of those programs that demands that you will talk EO (equal opportunity). You will talk sexual harassment. This one is where, as a team, you have an opportunity to talk about these kinds of ideas as they may relate to your job environment. How do you please the customer? How do you support the customer? What are the issues in your environment that are making it difficult to do what you need to do? What about differences of opinion and other conflicts? The unit has to lay out topics. They get together with the soldiers they work with—the ones they have to understand and know—and build on value-based team concepts together.

What we are really doing with Consideration of Others is an After Action Review (AAR)—a climate assessment of the environment. I'm not sure everyone has made the connection yet. Because the AAR process is routine for tactical operations, most people expect to have their opinions heard. AAR has taught us to listen and learn from different perspectives. It's a leader's skill. We do it every day. We just don't realize it. What is new in the Army is talking about the human issues. It takes practice. It took me about ten years to get comfortable saying what I truly felt. You want to fit in. You want to be part of the team—and part of it is seeing the team working. In retrospect, we might have done better as a team, in certain situations, if I had spoken up.

KEY POINTS: JAN SWICORD'S STORY

▶ An ongoing practice of assessment can renew a team's focus and approach to core values, as well as explorations of new ideas to improve the work environment and better serve customers.

▶ Regular dialogue strengthens a team's ability to effectively put their differences to work; it provides an opportunity for everyone to practice developing the leadership quality of enabling rich communication.

▶ It takes practice to talk about human issues, as well as business issues in a way that everyone is included and heard. Consciously learn to listen, learning about others and discovering that others' differences matter; it's at the intersection of your differences where the value comes through.

From education, corporate contexts, and the military, we've learned key points about the process of assessment, defining current realities from different vantage points. In summary, Bert Bleke taught us there is great value in putting our differences to work by first coming together. He also helped us recognize that what we have in common as leaders, regardless of business or organization, is people with the same wants. Sue Swenson pointed out that starting the assessment process with a senior leadership self-assessment helps you better understand yourself and your peer leaders, so that you can more effectively work together to put differences to work across the organization. And Jan Swicord reinforced that assessment, at best, is a day-to-day practice. It enables rich communication, provides an opportunity to discover and appreciate one another's differences, and creates a place to practice the Five Distinctive Qualities of Leadership. Here are a few ideas to help you put what you've learned into practice.

ASSESSMENT:
Strategy And Tactical Ideas

▶ **Examine your values.** Organizational values are the cornerstone of an inclusive environment that puts differences to work. Here are a few questions to consider: Have your organizational values been examined lately? Does everybody know what they are? Can everyone describe them? Are they manifested in all that you do as individuals and as an organization? How do your values express and support the Five Distinctive Qualities of Leadership? Do leaders and people talk about them, or are they just taken for granted day to day? Reserve time when your team meets; this could be virtually in a small group or a big town-hall type meeting. Pick one or two questions to explore together.

▶ **Discuss the Five Distinctive Qualities of Leadership.** Get together to explore the Five Distinctive Qualities of Leadership to make them your own. Start a blog or forum or even a series of virtual or face-to-face conversations to discuss them. Explore what they mean together, where your strengths are, where you need focus, and what you'll do about it. Welcome new ideas. Make them your own. Put them into practice at your rap session.

▶ **Assess who's in and who's out.** Find the cynics and skeptics holding you back from mastering putting differences to work as an organization. These two segments of your organizational community can have a significant influence on your progress in creating an inclusive environment that is positioned and skilled at putting differences to work to innovate, influence, and win. Find them in your organization. Watch their influence on others. Look for patterns. See how the organization has "rewarded" their behavior by positive and negative attention. Talk with them. These behaviors are often simply habits. See if you can negotiate them toward putting their difference and influence to work as a champion.

ASSESSMENT:
A Call to Action

> "Self-assessment is a process of self-discovery, a means for assessing even how to be: how to develop quality, character, mind-set, values and courage."
>
> —Frances Hesselbein
> Chair of the Board of Governors,
> Leader to Leader Institute (formerly the Peter F. Drucker
> Foundation for Non-Profit Management) and recipient
> of the U.S. Presidential Medal of Freedom

The call for regular self-assessment is not a new one. Common in the lessons passed on from the great sages, scholars, and doers has been the essential ingredient of introspection. Over two thousand years ago, Plato proclaimed,

"A life unexamined is not worth living." Lao Tzu also urged allowing regular time for reflection: "Turn inward and digest what has happened." And Gandhi left behind in his message that our real education comes from continually "drawing the best out of yourself." This is the return for our self-assessments as individuals and as organizations. We draw out the best in everyone.

One might conclude that self-assessment is the perpetual call to the leader to be keenly aware—always listening, reviewing, evaluating, interpreting, discerning, deciding, being—reaching toward the organization's mission, purpose, and values. Self-assessment is an essential component of change, renewal, and achievement for individuals and organizations. As we reach for new levels of innovation, leadership, and high performance requiring the fuel of differences, inclusion, and novel ideas, assessment must include examination of our capacity and capability in the human dimension of our leadership and our operations in order to drive success. Each bold action we take is always guiding us back to some form of self-examination in order to proceed to the next level. Involving and engaging people is the fastest way. The process need not be complicated or bothersome. For great organizations and great people, it is an integral part of life.

Start with questions with a focus on people.

Be grateful for the strengths you find in them.

Be truthful about what is standing in the way.

Reset your direction to tap into their collective talents.

Spend time examining your own behavior regularly.

Walk boldly!

Repeat these steps often.

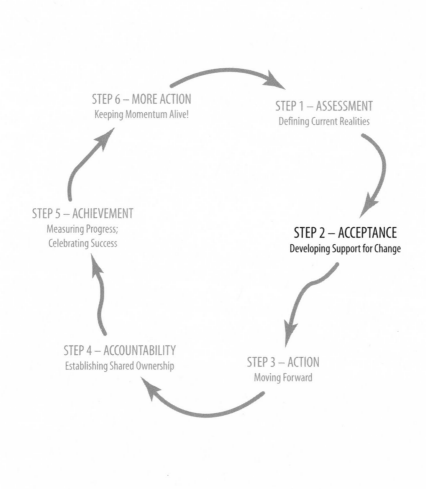

STEP 6 – MORE ACTION
Keeping Momentum Alive!

STEP 1 – ASSESSMENT
Defining Current Realities

STEP 2 – ACCEPTANCE
Developing Support for Change

STEP 5 – ACHIEVEMENT
Measuring Progress;
Celebrating Success

STEP 4 – ACCOUNTABILITY
Establishing Shared Ownership

STEP 3 – ACTION
Moving Forward

> "To create an environment which is conducive to breakthrough ideas, one must not exclude from the great mix—from the great diversity—because one of those ideas or those elements may, indeed, be the piece which sparks the next great innovation."

—Shirley Ann Jackson, Ph.D.
President, Rensselaer Polytechnic Institute,
speech delivered at IBM Watson Research Labs

CHAPTER 5

Step 2—Acceptance: Developing Support for Change

Like all types of change, it takes conscious effort for us to realize the benefits of putting our differences to work. Over time it becomes evident in new levels of innovation, new strides in leadership, and high performance from everyone in their own right, as we've been discussing. However, changing minds, and sometimes old habits, takes influence and practice. It also involves a well-thought-out process. A logical sequence might include defining current realities, figuring out what to do, taking action, setting standards for ownership, measuring progress, and celebrating results—everything we've plotted out as a course of action.

Just like any other kind of initiative, each important step of the human dimension of change, for the most part, is also driven by a process—a series of actions that begin the movement toward the desired result. Process comes easily for most of us. It is theoretical and unemotional. It looks good on charts. It can be made tangible with numbers, and it doesn't really ask much of us. So, typically, we are drawn to process *first*. It is comfortable and familiar. Unfortunately, too many leaders rely solely on process to lead change—and later blame its failure on the process, the mission, its execution, or the poor staff person who planned it. Unfortunately, this has been the cause of death of many people-focused initiatives. You may have experienced a few yourself.

Interestingly, the most critical success factor in leading change, the one that will create a culture that masters the art of putting differences to work, is often discounted, overlooked, avoided, or ignored—acceptance. Commenting on research on the *tactics of innovation*, futurist Joel Barker concluded, "It is natural and logical for people to resist change. New ideas upset the balance and change makes things difficult. Only by developing the ability to present your idea from the user's point of view will you be able to achieve success."

Gaining *acceptance* for putting differences to work as a key driver of success involves the following:

- ▶ Igniting interest and desire to lead in everyone
- ▶ Opening people's minds to seeing and valuing others' differences
- ▶ Creating new ways of working, thinking and exploring, solving problems, and creating new innovative solutions together
- ▶ Giving people an opportunity to learn about and practice the Five Distinctive Qualities of Leadership, and inviting them to tailor and refine them
- ▶ Helping people lift themselves above the obstacles of the past and present to see the benefits of differences working as drivers of success for them and the organization
- ▶ Facilitating everyone's discovery of how important they are

One of the advantages of pioneering a path is that if you "cut the brush away" on the new trail long enough, you bump into other kindred spirits. If you make investing and caring about others' success a practice, you not only get to explore ideas with others—and perhaps work together here and there—but also find yourself marveling over results they are achieving by encouraging people to put differences to work. It can happen right before your eyes step by step, year by year.

Grace Cathedral, a thriving place in San Francisco, serves as a shining example of how the fastest way to innovation, leadership, and high performance comes from a diverse group of people in a welcoming environment resonating acceptance.

One time earlier in the process of fulfilling its vision, The Very Reverend Alan Jones, Dean of the Cathedral, and I talked. We explored ideas about differences and acceptance. He offered a meaningful perspective that affirms what we can learn from one another when we meet on the common ground at that intersection of all of our organizational and individual differences:

ALAN JONES

A common theme in our culture is diversity and inclusion. The danger is in these words becoming mere slogans behind which we can hide, instead of our finding ways to help people see where social and personal stability really lies. One of the best analogies for a creatively stable society is an ecological system. The more diverse a system, the more stable it is. For example, fields of cabbage, after cabbage, after cabbage is not as stable as rows of onions, tomatoes, broccoli, and carrots. Unfortunately, far too many of us think of diversity as a threat. Actually, it is accepting the gift of our differences that moves us toward creativity and stability. Part of the discipline of leadership is helping people imagine and enjoy the "otherness" of others, seeing and delighting in its promise.

One of the ironies of life is that what we want most, we avoid most. I think that one of the great challenges for many people is to dare to be happy! True happiness requires that we accept the "burden" of our own significance. Each of us matters, and each of us is here to make a difference in the world. In the not-for-profit sector of society, particularly the church, we work to help people learn to accept themselves. Perhaps this work is not so different in a business, school, or community. On some level, we are all trying to help people learn to trust in themselves enough to serve others in some important way.

Diversity and inclusion are about the solidarity of the human experience where everyone has a unique place in what I call the divine ecology. No one is dispensable. What would it take to challenge and overcome our sexism, our racism, our homophobia, and our biases against newcomers toward those who don't speak our language? There is a lot of talk about family values—a good thing, depending on how generous one's vision is of this family. From my faith perspective, there is but one human family. We are all in a community where everyone—without exception—is respected. The message is: You are invited to participate, whoever you are. You matter and can make a difference in the world around you.

KEY POINTS: ACCEPTANCE

▶ Social and personal stability reside where differences meet in an environment of inclusion and acceptance, as a diverse ecological system is more stable.

▶ Part of the discipline of leadership is helping people imagine and enjoy the differences of others, learning through experience its advantages.

▶ We are all, on some level, whether we are in business, school, or a community, learning to trust ourselves enough so that we can effectively serve others in important and meaningful ways, putting our differences to work.

▶ Everyone has a unique contribution to make; the message is, You're invited.

What seems clear when we look at the notion of acceptance is that it is multifaceted and far-reaching. It involves personal acceptance of changing old habits and developing new ones. It asks us to open our mind and others' minds to more effective ways of conducting our unique businesses. In doing so, there is the *acceptance* of the abundant opportunities that exist at the intersection of all our differences—opportunities for us to grow, innovate, lead, and excel together far beyond what we can accomplish singularly.

Because this essential step is the least familiar to most of us, we have a great deal to learn from other perspectives from public, private and corporate sectors, including perspectives that span the globe.

First, there is a resounding need for all leaders of innovation, from the smallest community organizations to the largest businesses, to get a knowledgeable firsthand grasp and acceptance of the realities of the demographic change in the marketplaces, workplaces, and communities of the twenty-first century—not from an academic data standpoint, but from a deeper sense of personal connection that the Five Distinctive Qualities of Leadership can help put differences to work. So what's the business case, you ask? In a presentation at the IBM Watson Research Labs entitled "Powering Innovation through Diversity," Dr. Shirley Ann Jackson, President of Rensselaer Polytechnic Institute, shared that she has been calling for a national conversation on what she terms the "Quiet Crisis" to address the United States' capacity for innovation. In the following excerpts from her remarks, she also validates the belief that diversity drives innovation:

SHIRLEY ANN JACKSON

Because I lead a technological research university, I frequently address the topics of innovation and discovery, and my point is that diversity is a kind of energy—a power which generates the new, the unique, the innovative, the excellent. Diversity advances innovation to meet global challenges. Innovation is advanced by chance, by challenge, by choices, and by informed coincidence. It is nourished—it is powered—by the full breadth of diversity, and, overall, by the quest for excellence. Diversity is an energy which powers this quest.

...Innovation requires smart, focused people—drawn from the complete talent pool—challenging each other and understanding each other, to create something really new. And, true excellence requires drawing the best from all of us, through intellectual, gender, ethnic, and geographic diversity.

...Remember, diversity advances innovation; diversity powers excellence.

So where can we start as individual leaders? How can we establish a common reference point to advance our drive for innovation in our respective organizations, marketplaces, workplaces, communities, and nations by tapping into the wealth we have that resides our differences? How can you build acceptance and support for change?

Over the years, I've always found it helpful to go back to basics before taking off. It helps you rediscover that learning is finding out what we already know. Considering all the factors that will help us achieve the results, the basics about people rank high. So let's get back to basics to set the stage for the best practices and ideas about acceptance that follow.

THE BASICS OF ACCEPTANCE:
Men and Women Working Together

It isn't possible in this book to explore all the dimensions of differences that reflect who we are and all the issues that are inherent in our vast perspectives about them. So my idea is to apply what works well in solving any problem, to rise above the conflict and concerns to find our common denominator: the fact that we are men and women. Even after decades of work, the topic of gender differences remains a big one. In the last few years, as more and more women have entered the workplace, marketplace, and community to make their important contributions, the question seems to be shifting somewhat. I've witnessed it through our Women in the Lead Inspiration Blog (www .globaldialoguecenter.blogs.com/women) at the Global Dialogue Center and in emails I receive and in questions I've been asked during seminars. Instead of "How do I get ahead?" more frequently I am being asked, "How can men and women work more effectively together to innovate, influence, and achieve the higher-level results so much in demand?" There are, of course, some horrible stories of clashes between men and women working together. I've certainly learned many powerful, and sometimes painful, lessons myself over the years as a pioneering woman in leadership roles. Actually, there have been injustices and sad realities on both sides of the gender discussion.

What seems most productive for our exploration here in regard to putting our differences to work was to establish a reference point of the common ground we share as men and women. The goal is to assess how we can better accept one another, so that we can collaborate and cocreate a better future more effectively together. So I began to look at some of the studies and articles on the topic of gender differences across the world to satisfy this longing. I found there were plenty of studies and other information out there to consider. What surprised me was that much of it seems to stereotype our every behavioral difference and even all that makes us look different. This kind of data is perhaps interesting to ponder, but it seems to do more

WOMEN

Women have a remarkable capability to read people.

Women's style of management is based on sharing power
e.g., consultation, consensus, collaboration, inclusion.

Women are more interested in cooperation, harmony, and connections.

Woman feel more stressed with office rules they cannot bend.

Women are uncomfortable with an imposed leadership style.

Women want trust; they are more intuitive.

COMMON GROUND

"Men and women show NO difference in 'internal competitiveness' to meet personal goals and display excellence.

The twenty-first century may be the first in the modern era to see the sexes work and live as equals ."

—Helen Fisher
Anthropologist, Rutgers University, author, *The First Sex*

Men are more willing to endure exhausting workloads.

Men are more traditionalists; sensing and judgmental.

Men score higher in "external competitiveness."

Men tend to be direct – "I need your report by Friday."

Men tend to have difficulty sharing information.

Men deal well with hierarchy.

MEN

**Gender Differences
Meeting at the Intersection**

to separate and divide men and women than to help us discover how to work together using the strengths of our differences. One article from the UK by J. Bland entitled "About Gender: Differences" sums up nicely my initial frustration in finding a meaningful answer: "Men and women are different. That should be self-evident. They are different in aptitude, skill, and behaviour, but then, so is every individual person. So why do we make such a fuss about it?"

Two additional sources shed light in the right direction. One comes from Helen Fisher, a well-known anthropologist at Rutgers University and the author of numerous books, including *The First Sex: The Natural Talents of Women and How They Are Changing the World*. The other debates the question "Do men and women have different leadership styles?" published by the Cranfield School of Management in the UK.

As I pored over articles, study findings, and the information from the two sources just mentioned, every time I read about a unique difference about a man, *on average*, I flashed on a woman leader I knew with the same attribute; in other words, the same was true for women. For every characteristic attributed to women, *on average*, a man with the same traits came to mind. Some of the gender differences that stood out immediately are presented in the Gender Differences illustration.

What I found most encouraging in this exercise is if we combine all the attributes we each have as men and women, treating them as strengths, we have something powerful to build upon. This reality opens up great possibilities and real advantage for the kinds of collaborations we so badly need in every organization. Helen Fisher also offered encouragement when she concluded that men and women show no difference in "internal competitiveness" to meet personal goals and display excellence. Common ground!

The Cranfield School of Management "debate" with Susan Vinnicombe, director of the Centre for Developing Women Business Leaders, and Andrew Kakabadse, professor of international management development, also concludes that "gender isn't a significant differentiator in leadership performance." Again, another point we have in common. This specific comment highlighted an important truth about putting our differences to work:

> However, context—the culture of the company, the leadership style of the boss and the attitude in the office—does play a powerful role, citing that men and women in comparable jobs, in different organizations, respond differently, not because of differences and personality, but from the pressures established by leadership attitudes and behavior.

Here we can see the importance of creating not only diverse but inclusive work environments. Diversity multiplies the possibilities for generating creative new ideas, and inclusion creates an environment of acceptance for everyone. Additionally, it validates that it is essential to have buy-in from leaders at all levels who support diversity and inclusion. The need for leaders to develop the first two distinctive qualities of leadership is highlighted here: *Makes diversity an organizational priority. Gets to know people and their differences.*

THE FASTEST WAY IDEAS
FOR STEP 2—ACCEPTANCE

 Organizational Snapshot Prompter
Before filling your mind with others' ideas, take a quick
organizational snapshot. It will give more meaning to the
best practices stories, strategy, and tactical ideas that
follow (see the Resources and Studies section).

A great business case can be made when we consider the advantages of putting the strengths of both men and women together. Now imagine if we did similar comparisons across other dimensions of diversity—our unique differences. As we saw in the comparison between men and women, it seems logical that we would find a similar kind of result regardless of the differences we chose to compare. If we used decision-making methods or thinking styles, for example, we would discover differences in approach but common ground on which to build a meaningful collaboration. Let's look at three stories that teach us about the role acceptance plays—among one another, with our customers, within our teams, and within our communities—in being a catalyst for new levels of innovation.

Best Practice—Small Business

One look at acceptance comes from lessons learned from another trailblazer. The lesson here is learning how limiting sameness in a business can be. Nana Luz is the cofounder of Softype, Inc., an innovative business solutions company serving small to midsize companies in areas of business systems, Web presence, outsourced IT services and document management. It has teams working in California and Mumbai, India. Previously, Nana served as the founding CEO of Lotus Printing for sixteen years, where she created a whole new customer experience by putting differences to work with a team of global citizens. I had the opportunity to talk with her about her early lessons in building Lotus Printing, specifically about the implications of sameness in a business and her own discovery and acceptance that differences were the drivers of innovation and customer success.

NANA LUZ

Growing a business takes a willingness to see when things aren't working and to make changes. Lotus Printing was started in the summer of 1985 by two women who wanted to find balance—between home life and work life. It was practically impossible. Customers don't want to work with people who want to work two days here and three days there. We also had a lot more to learn about the process that we had not anticipated in order to serve customers. This took time.

The first few years were a struggle. I found several good people to work with. My idea was to have a company that would be completely women owned and operated—women running the presses, doing prepress work, answering the phones, estimating, and selling. I found this tremendously difficult. Not only was it difficult to find women to do these kinds of work, especially in the skilled areas, but I found there was a very different dynamic when there were all women working together. Additionally, in this particular situation, the work environment was anything but harmonious. The experience taught me my first important lesson: people have to work well in teams for a business to succeed.

In reflection, we became a very different organization with a community full of diverse people, and Lotus became its mirror image. Our team worked well together because of it. I never really pointed out that our workplace was incredibly unique—not even to our staff, but I think people knew it.

After you have a critical mass of diversity in your organization, more and more people somehow arrive. However, as I turned the reins over to other people, I had to work with those managers to make sure that suddenly everybody didn't become all the same kind again. I spent a lot of years developing the diversity we enjoyed at Lotus, because I think diversity brings vibrancy to a business. Maintaining diversity takes an ongoing consciousness about who you bring into your business. It doesn't happen by itself.

KEY POINTS: NANA LUZ'S STORY

▶ Serving customers means building an understanding, acceptance, and ownership for fulfilling their needs; they don't want to work with people that aren't available.

▶ Growing a business takes an awareness to see things that aren't working and a willingness and acceptance to change them.

▶ People have to work well at putting their differences to work for a business to succeed.

Building and maintaining an organization that thrives on the strengths of differences requires thoughtful attention by the leadership, as Nana Luz pointed out. Our traditional measures are perhaps somewhat limiting, as we continue to wake up to the value of the broader dimensions of diversity and the important role they play in helping you take the fastest route to innovation, leadership, and high performance.

Best Practice—Government and University Partnership

How can we learn to be more accepting of one another as men and women? Putting our differences to work often comes with an initial struggle. One story I've never forgotten demonstrates how this struggle can be transformed into groundbreaking achievement bringing about innovation, new levels of leadership, and high performance. It is a story told by Donna Shirley, former Manager of the Mars Exploration Program at the California Institute of Technology's Jet Propulsion Laboratory, also shared in her book *Managing Martians*. I met Donna when I was producing an HP Women's Conference in Colorado and was moved by her story of innovation and leadership:

DONNA SHIRLEY

It was an honor to manage the team developing the first automated Mars roving vehicle. The development of *Sojourner*, the Mars Pathfinder rover, included many functions, such as instruments, engineering measurements, computation and data management, communications, and more. We needed a team capable of developing all these functions. Since we couldn't afford a specialist in every area, we needed creative, flexible generalists. The team we built was a mix of researchers and experienced flight project people, old and young, male and female—a multicultural group with many distinctive sorts and types. We came to operate like a family. The advantage of a multicultural team like this is that the viewpoints of one culture are likely to be new to another culture. This newness is what fuels creativity that is reflected in the team's results. For us, part of the creative success was that the Mars Pathfinder team built and flew *Sojourner* for a total of $25 million, a new record for low-cost planetary spacecraft. On July 4, 1997, *Sojourner* landed on Mars.

There were many lessons about diverse teams learned on this project, as well as during my career spanning more than thirty years. One important lesson was that misunderstandings and misinterpretations of behavior mainly arise in the area of culture. One glaring example is the white-male-dominated business culture reacting against inclusion of women and minorities. If you join such a team, some people are going to be uncomfortable. For instance, I'm the classic "pushy broad." After more than thirty years in a male-dominated business, I became vocal, assertive to the point of aggressive, and, to some people, obnoxious. On the other hand, I have a lot of experience being overlooked or ignored if I'm not assertive. In recent years, I've mellowed—partly from being more personally secure, partly from being more accepted in the engineering establishment. Diverse teams must be open to differences and to the surprises that occur when people react differently than you expect. Everybody needs to be sensitive to how their style and behavior affect other people. Most of all, what is required to make it work is creating an environment of mutual respect.

KEY POINTS: DONNA SHIRLEY'S STORY

▶ Multicultural perspectives fuel creativity that reflects in results achieved.

▶ Misunderstandings and misinterpretations of behavior arise from our differences in perspective, work, life, and culture experiences.

▶ We have to learn how our style and behavior affects others; we have to be adaptable and willing to create an environment of mutual respect for everyone.

As Donna Shirley's story reflects, we are the creators of diverse and inclusive organizations, workplaces, marketplaces, and communities. Here we see a vivid example of how the Five Distinctive Qualities of Leadership open the way for success. Establishing a conscious goal of creating an environment where innovation thrives because of our differences is the beginning. Getting to know others, developing open, honest communication, personal responsibility and mutualism as the final arbiter—*everyone benefits; no one is harmed*—ups the ante for us all. At its best, we already admitted that putting our differences to work, at this time in history, goes beyond great teamwork. It also begins by developing a set of new conscious habits and behaviors.

Looking at the realities of our workplaces, marketplaces, communities, and the world today, some may think these kinds of people-focused ideas are not practical—or perhaps idealistic or even too simplistic—as remedies for such complex problems as those that exist today. These skeptics point out our own need to believe, accept, and try things that challenge us. I've talked with some highly respected intellectuals who balk at such simple ideas, as if talking with one another in dialogue and being good neighbors in both work and life were of little value or impossible to achieve.

I believe these reactions are symptoms and demonstrate key areas where we need to build acceptance. They're just our excuses—notions that limit possibilities and demonstrate our doubt and fears. They continue to keep us separated as people and fill our minds with limiting beliefs, which in turn keep us in a state of inaction. Even in the face of similar thinking, myself at times, I say these are excuses, because there are just too many examples that prove otherwise. The previous stories offer a number of compelling instances, but here is still another.

Respect the Divine and Love People.

—Corporate motto, Kyocera Corporation

Kazuo Inamori, chairman emeritus, Kyocera Corporation in Japan, personifies a legacy of achievement that sets an undeniable example for us, which is documented in his book, *A Passion for Success: Practical, Inspirational and Spiritual Insight* from Japan's Leading Entrepreneur. He tells us that it is passion that opens up new eras. He affirms that our most important duty as a leader is to infuse our energy into our people until they burn with passion. He also shares the advice given him from the man who originally funded his innovative success. The mentor asked just one thing from him: "Never be a slave to money." Heeding this advice and staying true to his personal business philosophy—"Respect the Divine and Love People"—led to great success, proving that *win-win opportunities compound synergy.*

Kazuo Inamori's conviction to uphold this request highlights the strength of the fourth distinctive leadership quality, *Holds personal responsibility as a core value.* It was the foundation upon which his success was built. His business philosophy endures today. It is that sense of personal responsibility within us first that helps us engage others and provides a new platform for creating an environment that thrives on a new philosophy of "I win; you win; we all win." Finding ways to reach the people in your organization, involving them in creating such an environment, means building acceptance, raising day-to-day consciousness, and helping each person contribute through his or her own behavior and actions.

Best Practice—Community Organization

As we work to make differences our strength, I have learned through my work at our Global Dialogue Center that organizations of all kinds have much to learn from one another. In the vastness of our differences in customers, products, and services, we do hold lessons learned that can be applied in any organization, as you've seen in some of the stories told so far. What we share in this human dimension of leadership are the firsthand experiences, the knowledge, and the wisdom we gain from working with people. Those insights hold secrets for our future successes as we meet at those intersections of difference throughout the world.

This truth was revealed to me vividly when Dr. Yehuda Stolov, Executive Director of the Interfaith Encounter Association (IEA) in Jerusalem, contacted me at the Global Dialogue Center. Dr. Stolov wrote me a kind, personalized letter to inquire if we would be interested in receiving IEA's newsletter. I wrote him back. As we corresponded, a compelling question was tugging at me: "What could leaders learn, across all disciplines and organizations, about this human dimension of leadership from an organization working so close to the well-known gaps of difference and misunderstanding?" From the stories I read, Dr. Stolov's organization was opening up avenues to put differences to work in ways that even the most powerful leaders in the world were struggling to do. What could we learn about how to cultivate acceptance of differences from IEA's example? I soon discovered and asked Dr. Stolov to share his story. See for yourself:

YEHUDA STOLOV

Some years back, I joined with a group of longtime activists in interfaith dialogue to form the Interfaith Encounter Association. Each of us felt a compelling need to make interfaith dialogue a widely used tool for building harmonious intercommunal relations in the Holy Land and the Middle East. Our vision was to make interfaith dialogue a real social movement—one that would transform these relations of mutual ignorance at best—and violence at worst—into mutual understanding, respect, and trust.

We started with a framework of inclusion from the start. Our Board was composed of two Jews, two Muslims, two Christians, and two Druze. These inclusive qualities attracted many people very quickly. We were moved by the response that included sharing thoughts, signing up for our mailing list, and thousands of people participating in hundreds of dialogue programs.

One of the most meaningful breakthroughs for me happened when we began a series of Israeli-Palestinian conferences. The early moments of the first conference started with hesitation and suspicion. However, quickly the two groups connected very strongly. A little more than twenty-four hours after meeting, we had a social evening. Small miracles took place. People were singing together. They were dancing together. They were telling jokes with each other. When the time came to say farewell, they were hugging each other and feeling sad to go back to the outside reality. It was really like Alice going into Wonderland and back.

After being involved in these interactive dialogues focused on building mutual understanding, respect, and trust, I believe real peace is possible and that it is much easier to achieve than one would think.

In 2006, Dr. Stolov was awarded the Seventh Prize for Humanity by the Immortal Chaplains Foundation in the United States.

KEY POINTS: YEHUDA STOLOV'S STORY

▶ Inclusion accelerates acceptance.

▶ You can transcend hesitation, doubt, and fear in a short time by getting to know people, learning about their differences, and sharing yours.

▶ Dialogue opens the way for putting differences to work; small miracles take place. Dialogue helps build a foundation of mutual understanding, respect, and trust.

Dr. Stolov's story validates that meaningful dialogue is a powerful catalyst for building acceptance and accelerating change. It is definitely a reliable vehicle for those looking for the fastest way to unite people and get going toward innovation, leadership, and high performance. Far too often in business organizations of every kind, as leaders, we stay an arm's length away from people. We commission consultant-conducted surveys to tell us what people think, instead of asking them ourselves and listening.

In their groundbreaking book *Follow This Path: How the World's Greatest Organizations Drive Growth by Unleashing Human Potential*, Curt Coffman and Gabriel Gonzalez-Molina document Gallup's research and conclude that engaged employees feel good about their jobs and themselves. They note twelve simple requests: "Focus me. Equip me. Know me. Help me see my value. Care about me. Help me grow. Hear me. Help me see my importance. Help me feel proud. Help me build mutual trust. Help me review my contributions. Challenge me." Eleven of these twelve seemingly simple requests from employees could be met or be improved with regular conversation with leaders. I don't think these basic human desires belong to employees alone. How about students, volunteers, and many more? Who of us doesn't long for such a sense of belonging from the organizations and communities where we participate and contribute? This was evident in Yehuda Stolov's story. Here again we see how the distinctive leadership quality of enabling rich

Follow This Path

Focus me.

Equip me.

Know me.

Help me see my value.

Care about me.

Help me grow.

Hear me.

Help me see my importance.

Help me feel proud.

Help me build mutual trust.

Help me review my contributions.

Challenge me.

Source: Follow This Path, "Steering toward Engagement," p. 95.

communication can become a powerful catalyst for developing acceptance and support for the strategies and goals you've established. It gets people connected.

ACCEPTANCE:
Strategy and Tactical Ideas

Here are a few ideas to help you put what you've learned into practice.

▶ **Change the experience of sameness.** If your leadership team is primarily a homogeneous collection of people, creating a more diverse mix may take time. One way to begin the process of everyone having the opportunity to practice *acceptance* and the Five Distinctive Qualities of Leadership is to look for ways to change their day-to-day experience now by integrating differences into it whenever possible. (1) If you have an all-male team, invite senior women from other companies or organizations to participate in a leadership dialogue session with your team. (2) Develop a multicultural advisory board. (3) Extend your management team to include business partners and representation from other alliances to change the mix. The fastest way to acceptance is through relationship and firsthand experience.

▶ **Reinvent how you work together.** One way to promote acceptance is to let people decide how they will work together with their differences. There is truth in the saying "Most people don't resist change. They resist being changed." Invite them to build a contract around the Five Distinctive Qualities for Leadership to create the platform for putting differences to work themselves, and the process will in turn begin to change them.

▶ **Take an inventory of your differences.** They say you can't really understand another's perspective until you have walked a mile in that person's shoes. Using the Dimensions of Differences illustration, invite everyone on your team to consider one or two differences they bring to your team or organization that they believe add the most value. Create opportunities for sharing. This could be at face-to-face meetings or in a virtual setting or utilizing some other Web 2.0 technology, like video or blog. This kind of knowledge exchange could be done all at once or as an ongoing focus, where you put the spotlight on one or two people at a time. Use the stories to set the frame for conversation and inquiry.

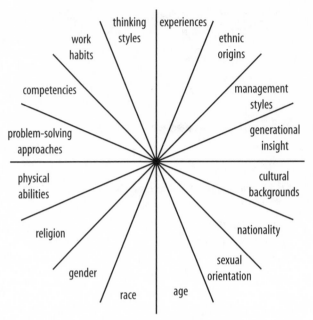

Dimensions of Differences

ACCEPTANCE:
A Call to Action

> "The future is built with the same courage we have
> to build the present. How can we unite?"
>
> —Adolfo Pérez Esquivel
> Winner of the 1980 Nobel Peace Prize

Developing support for putting our differences to work as drivers of success, or any other change effort, is a person-to-person job. Over the years, in working with other leaders to develop acceptance of oneself, each other, support for change, or to unite a group of people for some endeavor none of them could do alone, I've learned there are two critical elements that open the way to acceptance and support for change:

▶ **Have a compelling message.** This means knowing exactly what you
   want and need and why. It also means being able to present it in a
   few minutes in a way that sparks interest and gives any person a
   powerful reason to get involved—a request they cannot resist based
   on its merit.

▶ **Meet people peer to peer.** Regardless of whom you meet, be with them as if you were a peer. State your case with the countenance of leadership, not a self-conscious subordinate. Put your energy and passion into the message—and be as genuine as you would talking with a friend. Let your enthusiasm infuse people with your difference and your example.

While I was writing this chapter, I came across an anecdote in a book that belonged to my dad. Its lesson sums up what I am saying here: "When the world says, 'No,' your business is to say 'Yes!' and prove it." That is the key to gaining acceptance on any front.

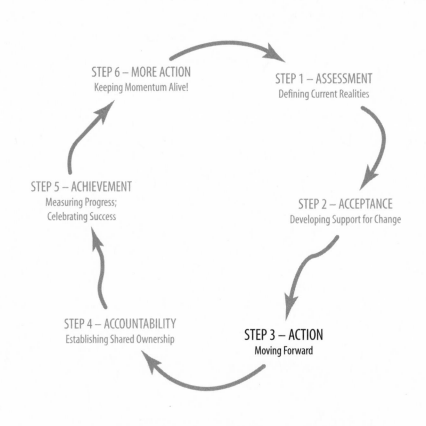

STEP 6 – MORE ACTION
Keeping Momentum Alive!

STEP 1 – ASSESSMENT
Defining Current Realities

STEP 5 – ACHIEVEMENT
Measuring Progress;
Celebrating Success

STEP 2 – ACCEPTANCE
Developing Support for Change

STEP 4 – ACCOUNTABILITY
Establishing Shared Ownership

STEP 3 – ACTION
Moving Forward

CHAPTER 6

Step 3—Action: Moving Forward

The primary action that will unleash the *idea power* in businesses and in society is dependent on putting our differences to work. As we are learning, for most of us this will require personal actions, including a shift in how we think, behave, communicate, take personal responsibility, and make decisions with everyone's interests in mind.

Moving into action challenges the best of us, because action itself is a paradox. On one hand, it is the hallmark that has preceded every innovation, act of leadership, and accomplishment since the beginning of time. Think about one of your own achievements, great or small. Remember that first important step forward. It was freeing, wasn't it? It felt good to be in motion. Heading in the right direction. *Doing*, at last!

On the other hand, at times even the most action-oriented find themselves temporarily paralyzed by the thought of taking action. Even very talented leaders sometimes get stuck. This happens many times after they have made a personal investment in taking a deep dive into the organization to assess where they are. It happens even after these skilled leaders miraculously pull off getting full sponsorship to proceed. Something happens. A hesitation. A panic over the feeling of vulnerability and risk of actually moving out, knowing you are holding the accountability for results. At this common occurrence, the excuses we come up with are often wild and many. This might not be a reality we openly discuss with others—or admit even to ourselves out loud—but I'm sure you've felt it yourself. It's that moment when your screen goes blank. The courage you bolstered up last week, convincing all your sponsors, disappears. The brilliance of the new people-focused strategy you designed and all those great ideas suddenly become suspect. The risk of mobilizing has great power over us and often helps us find a detour.

I was working once with a talented young manager, leading a business-directed change initiative with a focus on putting differences to work across a global organization. She had done an exceptional job in influencing bottom-line results over the period of a couple of years. The organization had reached a place where the senior leaders wanted to focus on one key issue—teaming up diverse sets of talent to better serve customers. They felt this creative concentration would boost customer relationships, while adding more value to their offering with a direct positive impact on business results. So they commissioned a group of senior managers to look closely at this specialized kind of collaboration and teamwork from the vantage points of their individual businesses across the world. The goal was to come up with a plan of action that put a new brand of excellence on teamwork to drive success. The senior leaders chosen were the "A-Team." The day we spent together resulted in analyzing each of their businesses, doing some computer modeling, and spending time in dialogue around how to effectively put differences to work throughout the organization. The plans for moving out were solid by everyone's admission. However, at the last minute, one leader suggested they pull together a "sub–task force" to study the issues and senior leaders' plan of action to make sure it would head them in the right direction. There was immediate consensus. The sub–task force they pulled together was huge, representing all their organizations worldwide. It took a whole year for them to make their analysis of the senior leaders' plan. When finished, they presented their findings, validating everything that had been concluded in the session that the senior managers had held one year earlier. The forward-thinking ideas were then *one year* behind in getting implemented.

Why is it that we so quickly take such a detour, rather than the bold action we know needs to take place? What is it that keeps us at the threshold of *doing* when it has so many benefits? All indicators point to one answer: Taking action requires more of us. It often requires paving a new path. Risking. Doing something we know little about or that maybe has never been done. So we often shelter ourselves with talk and task forces. Because the longer we talk, analyze, work to crystallize the perfect words to describe our unique issues (the bigger sounding and more complex, the better!), the longer we avoid having to *act*—having to figure out what to do, whom to trust—and then risk doing it.

There has always been the call for leaders to become more. The wisdom of Michelangelo sheds light on the true risk: "The greatest danger for most of us is not that our aim is too high and we miss it, but that it is too low and we reach it."

However, what is different about the notion of *action* today from what it always has been? A quick look at the state of need in almost any direction suggests there is certainly no place for a leadership practice of *shrinking* that takes us on detours well off the direct path. We can see the urgency for innovation, leadership, and high performance in every field needing our attention. This is a time to accept that *we* are writing the rulebook for this new era. This requires that we pay attention, so we can gain understanding of how the landscape is fundamentally changing every day. Every action and behavior has to be considered so that it is strategically and tactically aligned, so we aren't working against ourselves. Albert Einstein described three of the most valuable tools leaders at all levels have to "cut the brush" for new innovations. Leaders at all levels possess them:

"The only real valuable thing is *intuition*."

"Logic will get you from A to B. *Imagination* will take you everywhere."

"The only source of knowledge is *experience*."

We have to be courageous to reach beyond the traditional—take the best with us from all we have learned—and develop a new sense of curiosity and openness that lies in the potential of people putting their differences to work to change the course of history in the marketplaces, workplaces, and communities across the world. We hold the responsibility to build a future, where meaningful innovation in our respective products, services, and means of collaboration is governed by mutualism being the final arbiter. Imagine what we could do if leaders at all levels, in thousands of organizations, across the world, put their intuitions, imaginations, and experience to work at their full potential. Now, there is a vision!

RUMOR HAS IT, WE'RE READY TO TRUST OURSELVES

There are more and more indications that a growing mass of pioneering leaders wants to take responsibility and rely on our own knowledge, know-how, and judgment. Dr. Peter J. Nicholson, President of the Council of Canadian Academics, set the stage for us in a captivating message he delivered to The Fields Institute for Research in Mathematical Sciences in June 2006 entitled "Harnessing the Wisdom of Crowds: The New Contours of

Intellectual Authority." What he says speaks to all of us across disciplines, cultures, and generations. He sums up the realities of a new world we can't ignore. He also reveals how he fits into the picture and invites us to change with him, while imagining the promise of our choice to do so:

> People today are much less prepared to defer to the experts. But at the same time, we are being swamped with data and information—a glut that cries out for analysis and summary. So there's a dilemma. Who to turn to? Increasingly the answer is—Well, to ourselves of course, as individuals empowered by a world wide web that has rapidly evolved into a *social* medium. More specifically, it is a medium that today supports *massively distributed collaboration* on a global scale that—we can only hope—will help us make sense of it all.
>
> Let me say at the outset that I am not particularly comfortable with the future I foresee. I am, after all, a charter member of the "old guard" and will never really belong to the new. But I am also an optimist and a realist. The world has changed—*and so must we.*

Technology and the Internet are expanding the possibilities we have to put our differences to work in empowering new ways. As we learned in Part 1 with the Habitat JAM story, both differences and technology are accelerating the influence of our actions. New possibilities continue to unfold at breakneck speed. Are you on board yet?

"By 2008, almost 60% of organizations are likely to have some sort of social media program in place." These were the findings according to a well-documented 2007 global study, "How to Use Social Media to Engage Employees," conducted by Melcrum, a global research and training organization with a focus on internal communications (www.melcrum.com). The study provides an inspiring overview of the state of social media and how organizations are using it to connect with their constituents. It includes inspiring case studies from companies like Microsoft, IBM, and the World Bank headquartered in the United States; ING Group, BT, and Unilever in the United Kingdom; Atlana in Germany; and Nortel and the National Research Council Canada.

What is exciting about this Web 2.0 evolution is that there is an energy that comes with this new sense of freedom and connection—and companies are rapidly

Web 2.0— What Is It?

Online technologies and practices that people use to share opinions, insights, experiences, and perspectives with each other. Social media can take many different forms, including text, images, audio and video. Popular social mediums, include blogs, vlogs, message boards, podcasts, and wikis.

—*Wikipedia*

and wildly opening up new possibilities for collaboration we never imagined. This isn't something I've read about or studied in the distance. I am hooked myself and have been pioneering new ideas in virtual space for over a decade with our team, our Global Dialogue Center community, and also with customers. I heard a keynote speaker say not too long ago, "We've got to spend more time 'knee to knee' in dialogue." At the time, I was just opening the Global Dialogue Center, our online virtual gathering place for people throughout the world. At the time, I truly had no idea what was in store. More importantly, in just a few years, I marvel how social media in its various forms has transformed the idea of dialogue "knee to knee." I couldn't have imagined how it would change work and life as I have known it, while deepening my ability to serve customers and communicate, collaborate, innovate, lead, and reach for high performance in a whole new dimension.

THE GREATER IBM CONNECTION

One example of companies mobilizing to put differences to work is one of my new online communities: The Greater IBM Connection, a business and social collaboration network for IBMers, past and present. It is an exciting place bubbling with new ideas and opportunities for innovation. There are multiple ways to connect through Web 2.0 technologies, including its own IBM wiki, news, reports and briefings, a special group message center, a blog, plus opportunities for collaboration on innovative projects to make a difference. It also has a magnificent online 3D complex that is being built by IBMers at the Greater IBM Islands of Innovation on Second Life. It is an amazing place. Through Debbe Dae, my avatar at Second Life (depicted in the illustration), I attend events, meet other IBMers all over the world, and continue to see innovation from a whole new perspective.

IBM Innovation Center at Second Life.
Debbe Dae, a.k.a. Debbe Kennedy, watching an innovation video.

Whether it's attending a meeting in 3D or some other kind of a gathering of early explorers of this new Web-based dimension, you can't help but see and feel the potential for bringing talent together across the world. It is a more hip IBM, more open, with the friendliest people. You can sense that it is a "simmering pot" with a hearty soup being made with nearly unlimited potential for nourishing, nurturing, and engaging talented, innovative minds. In a very personal blog message on the Greater IBM Blog, Flor Estevez, Operations Manager and Producer for the Greater IBM Connection, shared the story of how the Greater IBM Connection was created. It started first by communicating with alumni, listening to what they wanted and responding. The ideas took the notion of an "alumni network" to a whole new collaborative adventure inside and outside IBM.

FLOR ESTEVEZ

This community didn't "just happen," you know. Before we launched the Greater IBM Connection, we hired a research firm and traveled to five areas of the world, asking former IBMers, like many of you, whether you would find value in a social and business network based on your IBM affiliation.

One of the first things we learned: you don't want to be considered alumni. You said you still felt an important emotional tie to the company and its people, your old colleagues, and maybe some still working here. So, we aren't an "alumni" group; we're Greater IBMers.... I love it when we correspond and talk; it makes everything feel more human.

As organizations and communities are pioneering such new ways to engage and connect with others, you and I—all of us—have to move out with a new boldness, consciousness, and openness in our actions, big and small. We have to find our own creative ways to put differences to work. We have to step up our curiosity and be willing to explore new ideas, to talk with one another through technology and other forms of collaboration that bring us together.

As we make our way further into the twenty-first century, two truths put the spotlight on the mobilizing force of action: The front runners will be those who *act* now. The organizations that will become the new breed of champions in their respective fields will be those that have built diverse and inclusive environments brimming with differences that reflect the people, the markets, the skill set needs, while mirroring the communities they serve. They will be organizations positioned to understand, relate to, and respond to changing needs, cultures, relationships, and situations that will be very different from what we can possibly even imagine at this time. All of this will be greatly influenced by sweeping changes in how we connect, collaborate, and solve problems.

Dr. Nicholson helps us set the frame for the action by describing the context symbolizing the new paradigm we all are experiencing: "This new framework is shaped by technology—primarily information and communications technology; by globalization; by post-industrial affluence; and by a culture which, as never before, celebrates and empowers the *individual*."

Then you better start swimmin'...
For the times they are a-changin'.

—Bob Dylan

THE FASTEST WAY IDEAS FOR STEP 3—ACTION

Organizational Snapshot Prompter
Before filling your mind with others' ideas, take a quick organizational snapshot. It will give more meaning to the best practices stories, strategy, and tactical ideas that follow (see the Resources and Studies section).

As you get moving, it is important to emphasize that one of the powerful realities about putting our differences to work is that doing so is a paradox. At first glance, it might appear that what is meant is for us to all join together in a fest of consensus. It does call for us to come together, but to the contrary, it invites us to arrive maintaining all that makes us unique—our own brand of diversity—including our thinking styles, approach to problems, experiences, intellect, views of the world, values, and our distinctive creative minds. This point is affirmed by James Surowiecki in his book *The Wisdom of Crowds:* "Groups are smartest when everyone in them is acting as much like an individual as possible... but in organizations there is a real tendency to try and stress consensus... which makes groups less intelligent." With this reminder as a backdrop, as you prepare to move into the action step of putting differences to work, remember the goal is to bring out the best in people—new thinking, new ideas, knowledge, and know-how—and, at best, to help one another.

The magic of mutualism is in the combining of elements that are very different to create new ideas that offer great advantage for all the participants. Don't forget: Without diversity, mutualism is impossible!

—Joel A. Barker
Futurist, filmmaker, and author,
Wealth, Innovation & Diversity

What could we learn about action, innovation, and putting differences to work from an individual leader, who saw new possibilities and was willing to brave new territory in virtual space worldwide, long before *Web 2.0* was ever coined as a term? What could we learn from a leader willing to devulge a mistake and the lessons learned? What could we learn from a corporate executive turned small-business owner about learning to trust people? The following stories serve as inspiring examples from three passionate leaders —innovators in their own right—who have made putting differences to work a key driver of their success.

Best Practice—Corporation

The budding of innovation began shortly after 2000. Dr. Sidalia G. Reel, Director of Diversity and Inclusion for HP, was an early trailblazer in using virtual space with the intention of putting differences to work across HP. She was then Manager of Diversity Education at HP, with a well-known, dynamic personal flair for bringing a wide range of diverse of people together and creating memorable experiences for everyone. She was on a mission to explore creative possibilities to expand HP's diversity learning portfolio beyond the traditional awareness classroom programs. I had the good fortune to be working with the organization as it continued to expand the influence of HP's diversity and inclusion initiative as a key driver of business success across the company. We teamed up for what became, unexpectedly, a thrilling "magic carpet ride" into a new frontier that changed us and a lot of things. It required us to put our differences to work, so we could enable a whole bunch of people across HP to do the same thing.

It began as HP's virtual classroom was beginning to catch on for presentations and meetings. After attending a few pioneering training adventures held by other trailblazers, I realized it was clear there was something there, and Sid Reel saw it, too. It was the opportunity to take the basic virtual classroom and bring it to life, creatively changing the human experience—from a one-way, "mute your phone and listen" passive experience, to a center for meaningful, interactive dialogue across the world at HP.

Instead of getting all wrapped up in complicated plans, we decided to follow the advice of Aristotle: "The things we need to learn, we learn by doing," a motto the Diversity and Inclusion organization had adopted to forge other new paths. Sid led the way by landing dedicated virtual space. We built a simple vision and plan: (1) build a distinctively branded virtual space to give it significance; (2) create a meaningful one-hour experience, using all the bells and whistles that the virtual classroom offered and engaging people from the start; and (3) inviting HP people to attend an interactive "open house" in three time zones across the world to introduce the opening of the "Global eSpace: HP's Center for Cross-Cultural Dialogue and Invention." Sid personally took over development of the content, getting the word out and handling the logistics. It was fun to watch her pioneering leadership passions at work, cutting the brush to develop this new idea herself—no delegation here.

> *There's no substitute for hard work.*
>
> —Thomas A. Edison

I took on the branding and development of the dazzling slides we agreed would be used to set the tone for something new and different—and we collaborated on the tiniest of details.

Sid wanted to ensure the first-ever dialogue event in virtual space was a role model of inclusion. So it wasn't a surprise when she invited HP's Diversity and Inclusion webmaster, Paul Schoemaker, to step outside his job description to join us as one of the facilitators for the *maiden voyage* to the Global eSpace and back. How could he resist? Paul took on some key parts, also adding his male voice to the mix. The blastoff to three time zones was like being in a virtual spaceship.

SIDALIA REEL

The first event can only be described as elating. I remember the surprise of watching some fifty, sixty, one hundred people log on from all over the world in an instant, managers and employees, coming to learn, share their ideas, and see what the new Global eSpace was all about. We used a beautiful world map to have participants show us where they were. Now this practice is quite common, but at the time, it was new, and there was something so moving about seeing all those dots show up on the map, representing people who wanted to connect with one another—and they did. People fully participated in a meaningful dialogue, exploring the questions, and weighing in on polls, and then spreading the word for others to check it out in our other events in different time zones that same day.

I loved observing in others the moment they realized the power of the eSpace. It was diversity and inclusion at its best with different perspectives, languages, and dialects and even learning from local colloquial phrases from across the world. The one I remember was a woman from the UK, sharing she thought the Global eSpace virtual open dialogue added a "bit of ginger" to the conversation. The whole concept transcended physical space to create a level of intimacy in the moment that sometimes is not achieved when a group of strangers are in a room together.

One of the assets of virtual dialogue is that it is a great equalizer. There is anonymity for those who need it and the opportunity to speak up and be heard. Today, the eSpace is an active place for dialogue. The advances in technology have greatly enhanced its capability—and we keep getting better at using it. Few remember its beginning, but it remains with me—a time when a small group of people at HP opened up a pathway across the world for us to learn more about one another.

KEY POINTS: SIDALIA REEL'S STORY

▶ Pioneering efforts in putting differences to work are not always recognized when the ground is broken; it takes time for new ideas to reach their potential.

▶ Virtual space is a new frontier still unfolding with powerful tools to connect us across the world. You can get a lot accomplished together in a short time, involving everyone. "Learning while doing" accelerates talk into real action.

▶ The building and launching of HP's Global eSpace is a shining example of the Five Distinctive Qualities of Leadership put into action. It began with diversity as an organizational priority. It enabled everyone to get to know others and their differences with rich communication. Personal responsibility was the fuel to make this experiment one that endured; it was a win-win-win for the people, the organization, and rippling influences across the world.

The best leaders find new paths and set the tone, the example, and the priorities. The next story shows how a leader's actions can have less-than-favorable implications but still pave the path for putting differences to work that bring valuable lessons.

Best Practice—Corporation

When we least expect it, people show up to have a lasting imprint on your leadership growth. For me, it started with an invitation to participate in a first-time-ever event designed to put differences to work sponsored by the Academy of Management. The academy called together twenty academics and twenty practitioners to spend a weekend exploring innovative possibilities for the future of management. It was a powerful gathering of people meeting at the verge of their differences. The two groups couldn't have been more different with, what seemed initially, a wide unspoken crevasse of preconceived notions separating us from one another. At first, we kept our distance, staying in our familiar groups. Through a rich dialogue and exploration of ideas, we came together and did remarkable work.

The special meeting was held at the world-renowned GTE training center and hosted by Jerrold V. Tucker, then Assistant Vice President, Learning Solutions, GTE Service Corporation. I didn't personally talk with Jerry until the last twenty minutes of this remarkable experience, but I had witnessed him in action. Since then, I've learned he is a pioneer of mutualism. He lives it in his coaching, sharing, and belief in and care about others' success and well-being.

When I was writing my Diversity Breakthrough! Series, he shared a story that has had a profound influence on me and others. It is a story in which many have seen themselves, because it mirrors happenings in some organizations today. What is unique is his willingness to tell the truth, expose the unintended consequences of straying from our values, as well as sharing three lessons learned from bolting into action and later having the opportunity to start again.

JERROLD TUCKER

Sometimes our major triumphs in leading change in organizations emerge from painful lessons. Often the most important learning comes from unexpected teachers. So it was for me at GTE's management development center. The center was out of control by any business measurement at the time. GTE had commissioned a study by a major consultant to assess what to do. The recommendations were in. I was brought in to turn the situation around—to implement the recommendations from the consultant.

On my first day, as Chief Learning Officer, we laid off nineteen people. If I had to measure the way I handled it, I would have to say it was poor. The methodology was to call people up to one of the conference rooms. The message was "Your job has been eliminated." Then we directed them into the next room to hear about their HR benefits, followed by security escorting them out the door. It was a terrible process. Most of all, the recommendations from the consultant didn't fit GTE. It is a family-oriented organization. Laying people off in this manner was not part of our culture. Afterward, the rest of the organization was paralyzed in fear. We reduced the budget. We reduced head count—but instead of making improvements, we set the organization back further.

This mistake took about two years to fix. We started by first changing our focus to customer service and making sure every person understood their important role in our success—every dishwasher, curriculum developer, waiter, administrator, housekeeper, manager, and faculty member. We tried simple, creative ideas, like job swap days, so at all levels we understood what and how we each contributed. What we did best was unleash the talents of our diverse team of people, a dynamic group representing over fifteen different countries and cultures. Together, they created one of the premier management development centers in the world. There were many leadership lessons learned. Three stand out: Listen to input, but decide for yourself what is right to do. Preserve human dignity in all situations. Put your trust in people, they have the answers.

KEY POINTS: JERROLD TUCKER'S STORY

▶ Sometimes major triumphs in putting our differences to work rise out of painful actions and lessons learned. Listen to input, but decide for yourself what is right to do.

▶ Preserve human dignity in all situations.

▶ Put your trust in people; they have all the answers.

Best Practice—Small Business Entrepreneur

When I first met Charles Blodgett, landscape artist and owner of the Burgundy Group, I was sitting across the desk from him at IBM. He was my new boss. I was considered an up-and-coming young leader. To me, he was a kind of wild and crazy guy with a bowtie. He was intense, spirited, and knew the business down to the tiniest detail. He was also fun, suspect of your every move and intention, and operated with a contentious style with everyone. Being a brother with four sisters, he also took an interest in me and earnestly tried to serve as mentor. He challenged me, chided me, inspired me, and taught me things about being an innovator I've carried with me all these years. I learned more about putting differences to work under his leadership than from anyone in my career—not so much because he was exceptionally good at it, but because it was necessary for survival.

Much later, I worked for him in a second tour of duty, and again, he taught me the value of meeting at the intersection of difference to drive the highest levels of excellence. Since he left IBM, he discovered new meaning in putting differences to work as a small business entrepreneur. I had the chance to talk with him about his personal leadership transformation and what he has learned in the process. Sometimes the action we need to take to reach others different from us is first personal. Chuck teaches us that as leaders change, that evolution opens the way for us to engage people at a whole new level:

CHARLES BLODGETT

Sometimes the greatest learning comes the second time around. A few years ago, after retiring from IBM, I started a second career. My company is located near Atlanta. The Burgundy Group specializes in creative, innovative landscaping. After an experience I had working to build houses for the poor in Mexico with my church, I decided that my new business would employ Mexicans who are new to the United States, who were struggling to support families.

Over time, I recognized how valuable this experience has been for me as a person. I have always been a great talker, and suddenly I had to learn to listen more and communicate differently with my employees, who spoke only Spanish. Without having all the verbal communication, I find that the outcome is even better. There is a great deal more eye contact between manager and employee—and a feeling that you are in sync. You have to really pay attention to each other. You learn to convey you are pleased with what they are doing or to read whether they are trying to please you. You find understanding without talking about it. In a short period, a very strong trust is built. Somehow, we soon understand how we benefit each other by what we do. I provide an opportunity and good working conditions. They do excellent work. It doesn't take long to become simpatico.

As an IBM manager, there was never an assumed trust on my part. As an employee, you had to earn it from me—and because I was the manager, I expected people to come to me. In this business, I have had to trust people because I can't talk about what I want or always be with them with several jobs going at one time. In my entire IBM career, I was incapable of just letting people go—creating a common understanding of our mission and then allowing people to do their best. I always had to be in control—or wanted more control—or thought my ideas were better. Maybe the change has come from a combination of things. I've mellowed. I've learned people work best if given some freedom. Also, my employees have been great teachers. They taught me to trust.

KEY POINTS: CHARLES BLODGETT'S STORY

▶ Effectively putting differences to work is a human process built on trust; sometimes the first action you take begins by changing yourself.

▶ Getting to know people requires more than words; you have to find ways to synchronize your differences to reach for new levels of excellence together.

▶ *Mutualism* as the final arbiter for your actions and decisions creates a win-win-win: You win. I win. The customer wins with rippling influences to others all around you.

In all three stories, we can see the Five Distinctive Qualities of Leadership shine through the actions of each of these leaders. As we all work to carve out our important contributions in the global community of the twenty-first century, we are its pioneers. The foundation we lay for putting our differences to work in creating diverse, inclusive organizations, workplaces, marketplaces, and communities across the world will indeed shape our own lives and work, as well as the lives and work of others now—and those who follow us.

As the possibilities for innovation, leadership, and high performance become clearer, futurist Joel Barker's insight describes the nature of this pioneer's journey. At one poignant moment in his film *Paradigm Pioneers*, he is standing at Independence Rock in Wyoming, revisiting the one-third point going west on the Oregon Trail. The names carved into the granite echo the courage of the pioneers who opened the way for all of us. Joel concludes, "It's one thing to sit in your easy chair and watch the future being conceived in the distance. It is quite another thing to load up your wagons and help in the labor of its birth."

ACTION:
Strategy and Tactical Ideas

Here are three ideas to inspire your action that can be cultivated both virtually and in person. Together they demonstrate how simple ideas can be, how they can be integrated into day-to-day business with a productive purpose, while planting the seeds for building relationships, developing people and helping them practice putting differences to work.

> ► **Keep tactics simple.** The best-laid plans get changed. Much time
> is wasted in analyzing and creating elaborate plans for creating
> diverse, inclusive organizations. Elaborate plans often produce
> disappointing results. Like any business planning effort, you can
> only focus on a few actionable goals at a time. Select two or three
> specific goals, establish a doable target date(s) for completion (a
> little stretch is good), and put your heart into achieving them. Don't
> allow failure to be an option. Review what you learn. Do more.
> This approach works for many reasons. What you can see, you
> can achieve. What's doable is not overwhelming. What you put
> your heart into achieving remains a priority. Action results in
> progress. Your success in meeting a few specific goals will build
> your confidence and fuel action for next steps—what you need
> to do next will become clear in the process.

▶ **Make it *cool* to get involved!** Ask the people to help you figure out how to put differences to work more effectively in your organization. Use the Five Distinctive Qualities of Leadership to set the framework for their thinking and action. If leaders are engaged and involved themselves, it sends a message of importance. By involving others, you accelerate the acceptance process, and having a united group mobilizing is a powerful force.

▶ **Learn to listen; learn to trust.** Committed people get involved. So how do you foster commitment? A Saturn assembly team, when asked, "What's the first thing you would tell a boss to do to get commitment?" reportedly responded in unison, "Tell them to listen." To keep things interesting, use a variety of different formats. Here are a few ideas: (1) Try one-on-one and small-group conversations. A little personal time with people goes a long way in helping you know people better, imprinting positive messages, and—most important—listening to what they have to say. (2) Incorporate social media into your people communications plans (e.g., virtual meetings with you, blogs, and forums). These new technologies are proving to have great benefits for improving employee engagement, fostering internal collaboration, building internal communication, and creating two-way communications. This may be a new avenue for you, but over time, we'll all become masters of new forms of communication that make it possible for us to put differences to work. (3) Set up telephone hot lines that offer both anonymous and two-way replies.

ACTION:
A Call to Action

❝The journey of a thousand miles begins at your feet. ❞

—Lao Tsu

A big part of putting our differences to work begins with a first action. The unique translation above of Lao Tzu's well-known wisdom reminds us and also places the responsibility where it belongs—with each of us.

One of the most meaningful gifts that technology has afforded to those working in virtual space is that it sometimes allows us to take that action step that connects us across the world with people we were destined to *meet*. With Wendy Luhabe, Chancellor of the University of Johannesburg, our meeting was just a brush by one another in passing. She was a keynote at the ec06 Conference in Zurich, Switzerland. The Global Dialogue Center sponsored and hosted a preconference online dialogue on corporate responsibility and socially responsible investing with conference keynotes. Wendy was not able to attend, but we connected through email, finding common ground. I learned of her remarkable record of achievement and influence as what she terms a "social entrepreneur" with honors, including being named one of the fifty leading women entrepreneurs in the world in 1999 and recognized by the World Economic Forum as a Global Leader for Tomorrow. She also authored a wonderful book entitled *Defining Moments: Experiences of Black Executives in South Africa's Workplace*. It is from this contribution that I draw for this call to action.

In the front of her book, Wendy wrote a personal note to every reader in her own hand. It begins:

> I offer this book to help you appreciate that as we embrace the knowledge economy, what will really give substance to it are the personal and life experiences of each of us. They offer a perspective that moves the world to an economy that has a human face, an economy where the value of people, not just their minds, matters.... Our real value lives in our hearts.

As I have taken in her message and the stories she shares in this work, it has again caused me to sort through a lifetime of actions, big and small, in many aspects of my life and work. I see a common pattern in the experience of fulfilling a goal. There were visions of success that ignited passion. There was a lot of hard work, learning, risk taking, and mistakes. There were supporters greatly appreciated—*of every sort and type*—and dissenters to convince across many dimensions of diversity. There was always a firm belief in possibilities in the face of passing adversity. There was a deep sense of drive to make a difference. In the end there was the thrill of victory but rarely a cheering crowd. It was, instead, a moment in time when things felt really good inside. In the end, fulfilling a goal was most often a new beginning, not a finish. There were always new hopes that led to the next challenge.

I felt this pattern in the stories in Wendy Luhabe's book. One case study, entitled "Investing in People," really touched me. The insightful closing message, although written for South Africa's leaders, speaks loudly to us all across the world, as we work together to make our important contributions in putting differences to work for the good of all:

> Ultimately, as human beings, we are more inspired by witnessing our own people achieve levels of success that seemed unattainable. These are the pioneers and every society has them. Pioneers can have two entirely different effects on a society. They can unlock momentum

that motivates a greater number of people to success despite obstacles. Alternatively, they can make people less capable and more inadequate. The challenge for us in South Africa [and nations everywhere in the world] is to cultivate a culture where greater numbers of us are inspired and encouraged by the success of others to achieve our own, to make ourselves willing mentors, coaches and sponsors for those who follow in our footprints.

It was in this reflection of South Africa's leaders that I realized, if we could meet and talk about your experiences of taking action, we would also find a similar pattern. In fact, if we stopped to examine the most meaningful actions that have changed the world, we would also find common ground. Why? Because this is the journey of problem solvers, change leaders, and difference makers, past and present. *Keep going!* Your organization and the world need you.

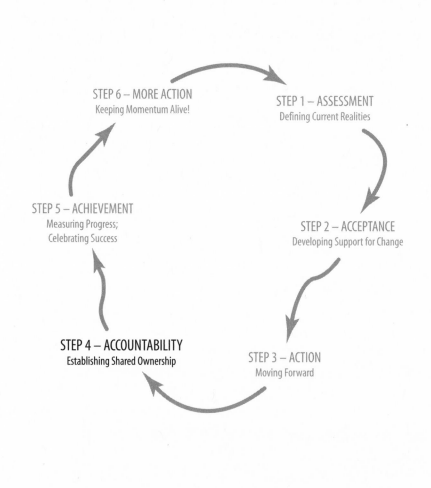

> "Diversity stretches our comfort zone, our conviction that there is only one way to do things. It gives our minds a larger stage to play on and demands agility in performing our roles."
>
> —John O'Neil
> President, Center for Leadership Renewal,
> and author, *Paradox of Success* and
> *Leadership Aikido*

CHAPTER 7

Step 4—Accountability: Establishing Shared Ownership

Accountability for creating a diverse, inclusive environment that effectively thrives on putting differences to work is an act of commitment. It reaches well beyond our talk and good intentions. It says we are expected to deliver. Do our part. Become involved. Set an example. Change our ways. Embrace new thinking and new people. Adjust our policies and practices—live up to the values we espouse. For most of us, this level of commitment touches us in a sensitive spot—*Can I? Will I? Where do I begin?* Consequently, perhaps without much conscious thought, a good many us have become very clever at finding ways to avoid being accountable. We deny we ever made such a commitment or justify the excuses aimed at explaining away what we didn't do. If this weren't true, wouldn't we be much farther along in having workplaces, marketplaces, businesses, and communities that welcome and value all people? How do we assume that distinctive quality of leadership that holds personal responsibility as a core value in all our work and contributions?

What is interesting is how we so easily shy away from the notion of personal responsibility. The common response to even the word *accountability* demonstrates this. Bring it up in a meeting and watch the immediate push-back by some—"I think we need to let people get used to the idea before we really put teeth into it." Or there are often attempts that keep us just short of making a promise—"We will set a goal of increasing diversity on our board, but let's not define what we will do about it just yet." Or, "I know we're focusing on making differences drivers of our success, but for this assignment, I want to stay with our insider team." Equally interesting is the mystery behind why we hold back our commitment. Think about it. Without accountability, why bother establishing priorities and goals, if there is no expectation to deliver results? We don't have to look far to see the results of a society where accountability and personal responsibility have somehow been lost in the shuffle.

Dr. Alex Pattakos, author of *Prisoners of Our Thoughts: Viktor Frankl's Principles for Discovering Meaning in Life and Work* and principal of The Innovation Group in Santa Fe, New Mexico, adds a unique perspective on personal responsibility:

> The *search for meaning* is a "megatrend" of the 21st century and is becoming increasingly important both for organizations as they redesign their impact on customers, employees, and society as a whole, as well as for individuals as they search for the deeper meaning of their work and in their everyday lives. Viktor Frankl reminded us of the personal responsibility that accompanies this new direction when he wrote of his own experience: "It did not really matter what we expected from life, but rather what life expected from us. We needed to stop asking about the meaning of life, and instead to think of ourselves as those who were being questioned by life—daily, hourly. Our answer must consist, not in talk and meditation, but in right action and in right conduct. Life ultimately means taking the responsibility to find the right answer to its problems and to fulfill the tasks which it constantly sets for each individual.

Accountability is not only about personal responsibility. It carries our commitment. In a drawer full of old papers I was cleaning out recently, I found a folded-up flip chart from a course I taught at IBM long ago. In big red letters across the top was the word *commitment*. Underneath were the insights I had felt important enough to keep. I searched to find the author and discovered that the first line is attributed to Abraham Lincoln. The rest we'll have to say has been passed along leader to leader. I think the message clearly defines the essence of the level of accountability and personal responsibility we are striving to reach as we practice the Five Distinctive Qualities of Leadership and take ownership for putting differences to work:

Commitment

Commitment is what transforms a promise into reality.
It is the words that speak boldly of your intentions and
the actions which speak louder than your words.

Commitment is making time when there is none.
Coming through time after time, year after year.

Commitment is the stuff character is made of.
It is power to change the face of things.
It is the daily triumph of integrity over skepticism.

As we move farther into the new millennium with a global marketplace, distributed global workplaces, and the needs of our communities throughout the world calling for our attention, we all have a lot of work to do. We need to recast our thinking about accountability for valuing diversity and building cultures of inclusion. This new thinking and these new actions will come from us—*not* "them." At best, we need to reshape it into a model of shared ownership—one that gives everyone a part in it and uses everyone's talent and new ideas to solve our most pressing problems. It means reevaluating our philosophies, policies, practices, and personal leadership. It means putting them to work to create an environment of inclusion far greater than we know today.

How do you stack up? Learn from others and explore possibilities for accelerating change in your organization by making it everyone's responsibility to put differences to work.

THE FASTEST WAY IDEAS FOR
STEP 4—ACCOUNTABILITY

 Organizational Snapshot Prompter
Before filling your mind with others' ideas, take a quick organizational snapshot. It will give more meaning to the best practices stories, strategy, and tactical ideas that follow (see the Resources and Studies section).

As I selected best practices to share for accountability, the task seemed to call for individuals whose leadership behavior and actions bring the word *accountability* to life from a number of vantage points. For this reason, the best practices shared focus on a pragmatist's business point of view, an educator's insight about how accountability starts within us, and the view of a leader who has pioneered putting differences to work, highlighting the important roles both personal and collective responsibility plays in achieving success.

Best Practice—Medium-Size Business

When it comes to straightforward thinkers and doers with high integrity, Sue Swenson, President and CEO for Sage Software—North America, ranks high on the list of exemplary leaders. I introduced her in Chapter 4, but here again her pragmatic style of executive people-focused leadership sets the tone for the important role accountability plays throughout an organization.

SUE SWENSON

We may be in different businesses, or perhaps you are in a very different kind of an organization. However, what I know we have in common is a purpose, a set of customers we serve and people we care about. If you are really serious about creating a culture that values people, you have to help everyone understand their role in it. It isn't something you can create on your own.

I am a pragmatist—and I must admit a fanatic when it comes to fairness. Shared accountability in all aspects of our business is a fundamental belief for me. Personally, I don't really spend a lot of time on diversity and inclusion as a program. As a practice, I don't do disconnected programs and separate launches of initiatives. I have been on the receiving end of such headquarters-driven programs. My belief came from this experience—I'm sure many of you can relate. As a young manager, I was trying to make things happen for the organization, yet I was continuously asked to put energy into new programs. If I had responded to every one, I would have been killing myself trying to deploy hundreds of initiatives—doing none of them well.

The approach I've taken as a leader is to personally take responsibility for finding ways to engage the organization—integrating fairness, openness, diversity and inclusion into our strategies, measures, recruiting practices, new hire orientation, management training, employee development, recognition programs, and our common protocol of behaviors and expectations for everybody. What has convinced me that this approach works is the results achieved. Clearly, you have the multiplication of your whole organization's energy and focus when you build it into the culture of the organization. The most gratifying part of this built-in approach is watching people embrace these principles—and do it because they find value in it.

The real accountability lies within the people—all of us as leaders and as individuals. Each of us has to find our own way to increase shared ownership in our respective organization, business or community.

KEY POINTS: SUE SWENSON'S STORY

▶ Take personal responsibility for finding ways to engage the organization, integrating fairness, openness, diversity, and inclusion into our strategies, measures, recruiting practice, new-hire orientation, management training, employee development, recognition programs, and behavior expectations.

▶ The integrated approach to diversity and inclusion helps everybody embrace its principles day to day.

▶ The real accountability lies within the people—all of us as leaders and individual contributors.

Expanding shared ownership often begins by figuring out where you need the emphasis and who needs your help. In *The Wisdom of Teams*, Jon Katzenbach and Douglas Smith sum up why the integrated "shared vision" approach Sue Swenson describes is so effective, because it instills the goals and expectations into everyone's consciousness through dialogue and practice: "Working visions work because they are heard in daily conversations and their impact is seen in the eyes and on the faces of people—not because they hang as plaques on the wall."

Best Practice—Education

I also introduced Bert Bleke in Chapter 4. His experience as a school superintendent provides a unique view of accountability from a leader's point of view. It transcends the boundaries of any differences we might see in our business or organization. He points out that a leader has to be accountable for establishing the vision, leading the way, and thinking long-term to build a new culture. His wisdom provides a framework for leading change for the long term that works for putting our differences to work anywhere you find the opportunity to make a difference.

BERT BLEKE

Somehow, I doubt many businesspeople think they can learn much from the schools. As an observer, a message I think we could pass on is that sometimes what it takes to make a difference is the passion and willingness to get the job done over time. If I have a problem with business in the last couple of years, it is that they appear to be obsessed with short-term results. "What is my next quarter going to bring to me?" You can't change a culture or make a difference with short-term thinking.

If you want to change a school, a workplace, an organization, or a community, you have to have patience. Change takes time. More importantly, character, diversity, and inclusion have to be supported at the top of the organization, because if there is a sense that it is not valued by the leadership, it is very, very difficult to achieve. Once the leadership foundation exists, there are some general principles that work for all organizations:

- Identify the non-changing core values on which your organization will succeed. At its heart must be the value you place on your people.

- Define your vision and direction. What is it your organization will accomplish? No vision—no direction—no goals simply means any path will do.

- The rest is process—assessing where you are now, working to get others involved, taking action, and finding ways to help everyone make a difference. It is diligence, courage, passion, and patience that will keep you focused on the long term—managing it in such a way that when you are gone, what you've tried to do will live on.

- If you really want to be a great manager and great leader of change, you need to look at the long term at what you are trying to accomplish for the good of the organization and everyone in it. Then kind of quietly go about your business, working with people and through people to get the job done.

KEY POINTS: BERT BLEKE'S STORY

▶ You can't change a culture with short-term thinking; you've got to be accountable for finding a new path that endures and will live on when you step away.

▶ The non-changing core values guide the way; they will be your "yardstick" by which you measure the value you place on your people.

▶ No vision—no direction—no goals simply means any path will do; your role is to get others involved and find ways for everyone to make a difference.

Best Practice—Corporation

Innovative leaders commonly bolster their courage and determination with an eye focused on the big picture—the long view as we learned from Bert

Bleke in the last story. This is an essential practice when working to put differences to work. Sometimes, leaders help plant seeds of good that take time to cultivate and sprout. Often they walk softly and quietly, spreading their influence where they know it will contribute to the *end* they have in mind. Innovative leaders aren't always known for their bold public contributions. More often, they see a small change behind the scenes that adds meaning for the people—a change that others overlook in a rush. No fanfare. Just *action* and *accountability* for what's *right* to do. After watching Cindy Stanphill, Director of Diverse Talent Development Programs for HP, operate for over a decade, I recognize these qualities in her work.

My experience of Cindy as a leader is that she looks out for what works— and if it doesn't, she gets it fixed. I remember how her sense of personal responsibility ended up clarifying a key message for the whole company.

A corporate slogan claimed, "Diversity drives creativity, invention, and business success." Cindy immediately saw the missing link—*inclusion*. Her thinking was diversity without an inclusive environment to support all the differences is ineffective. She didn't object to the slogan. She just boldly went to work to get it fixed and then went about using her quiet influence so the word would spread in all the right places. Reflecting on that moment in time, in the next story Cindy teaches us a key point about diversity and inclusion. She also shares an example of her experience in witnessing how diversity *and* inclusion work to drive creativity, innovation, and business success.

CINDY STANPHILL

What was missing from the original words—"Diversity drives creativity, invention, and business success"—was the important role *inclusion* plays. As many of us have learned, you can have all the diversity you want, but without inclusion, diversity can create chaos and not necessarily be value-added. I made a few modifications to the statement: "Diversity *and inclusion* drives creativity and productivity, which drives innovation and high performance, which leads to business success." I thought this made more sense and really captured what we were trying to do across the company.

What gave the words significance was seeing them in action. What comes to mind first is the "diversity search conference" our organization held a few years back. It was no ordinary three-day conference. It spawned all kinds of creative action plans, including ideas like having a community symposium on diversity, where General Colin Powell, former Secretary of State, spoke. The experience generated lots of enthusiasm, and many innovative ideas were transformed to realities that still exist today.

From the shared experience, a new strength and conviction about diversity and inclusion's important role in our business emerged. It is

Business Success

▲

Innovation and High Performance

▲

Creativity and Productivity

▲

Diversity and Inclusion

**HP Business
Success Process**

heartwarming to me to see that our managers and employees recognize the importance of diversity in our workforce. It has shown up in their behavior and actions in good times—and even in trying times of unexpected change.

Two important lessons stand out. One that I've frequently shared with others is the importance of *listening* to those with whom you think you disagree. In this work, there are often very polarized conversations around issues that people hold very close to them; many are very personal. I always assume that people come with good intentions. I find by listening with an open mind and spirit, I not only hear a new perspective but pick up pieces of wisdom that I can incorporate into my own thinking. I don't always agree with everything each person says—and I find the right time to speak my truth and have my voice heard. What has been valuable is that taking in others' ideas have made me a more innovative leader. It has also helped me truly value the differences everyone brings to the table. For this I am grateful.

The second learning for me has been to constantly looking at the *big* picture. It's very easy to get discouraged and give up if you are only looking at a small piece of the puzzle. When you step back and see the collective change, as well as understand and acknowledge the strengths that you brought to that change, it allows you to refocus, knowing any setbacks can be overcome. As a practice, I choose to put my energy and focus into what has worked well—always looking for an opportunity to innovate—rather than focusing on what may seemingly be going wrong at any given time. These are strengths I regularly call up to move forward.

KEY POINTS: CINDY STANPHILL'S STORY

▶ Sometimes accountability shows up as a leader's quiet influence to make things right to support the end in mind in the big picture.

▶ Helping others experience the value of putting our differences to work and ensuring it has an enduring influence reflects a leader's willingness to be accountable for results achieved.

▶ Listening to others' ideas and perspectives is a great source for learning and personal growth. Keeping your eye on the big picture and what works helps you find where to spot the opportunity to innovate.

ACCOUNTABILITY:
Strategy and Tactical Ideas

Here are three strategy and tactical ideas to help you consider how to incorporate the important action step of accountability with leadership influence, integrating putting our differences to work in mainstream processes and owning the words and the vision.

▶ **Give the focus on people clout and influence.** Setting expectations with specific people leadership objectives in manager performance is becoming more common, at least in large organizations. This is the easy part. One might assume that putting people leadership on a par with mainstream business objectives and then consistently following through with accurate evaluations is rare—and, indeed, many organizations don't set these kinds of expectations at all. Remember, putting differences to work is the fastest way to innovation, leadership, and high performance if you, the leader, set the framework of success through your own actions and behaviors.

▶ **Integrate: eliminate the not-so-obvious inhibitor.** Often many subtle actions have far-reaching implications for consciously building an organization that puts differences to work effectively by integrating accountability into mainstream business practices—for example, attracting, hiring, developing, promoting, and retaining top talent. These subtleties do not show up in reports. Sometimes they are so ingrained in the organization's culture or within certain powerful individuals that they are not easily detected in a cursory review— they show up in results (or a lack of them). The best way to build accountability for results into your culture is to step back and look at the big picture. Here are six indicators to watch for:

- Your board, senior leadership team, and up-and-coming talent remains primarily homogeneous after numerous opportunities for change.

- Meetings and events have only a homogeneous group of presenters.

- Key positions are filled with *clones* after repeated opportunities to bring in more diverse perspectives.

- Women, people of color, and anyone representing a difference, although highly competitive, frequently come in *second*; when hired, they are put in positions without supportive, involved sponsors.

- Women, people of color, or other different *sorts and types* are unintentionally, but repeatedly, overlooked when spontaneous "inner circle" meetings and gatherings are held.

- Those in power often, but subtly, use intimidating, thoughtless language and behavior to keep new ideas and new perspectives from influencing the status quo.

▶ **Own the words and the vision.** Although the terms *diversity* and *inclusion* have been defined and interpreted by many, they still remain misunderstood and have no real meaning for some. Actually, the only definition or interpretation that matters is the one your organization has adopted or created. If you want everyone in the organization to buy into putting differences to work and diversity and inclusion are core parts of it, invite them to have an influence on what these important words mean to your organization. Encourage dialogue, so that different parts of your organization can decide for themselves what ideals define a diverse, inclusive organization that puts differences to work from their unique vantage points. There may be variations on interpretation across the organization as a whole, but if they are grounded in the same values, the differences will be minor. What's more important is that the words belong to the people. A collection of their uniquely crafted interpretations would provide great insight into the thinking of the people in your organization across disciplines, geographies, and functions. Share them. (Create your own book of insights— it could be a best seller!)

ACCOUNTABILITY: A CALL TO ACTION

"Hey, brave heart, how you read my troubled mind....
You are the "I" for the dot; You take no prisoners for your
thoughts;... You're like the sunset that reflects hope for
all mankind. "

—Jeff Pasternak
Singer/songwriter, *"Brave Heart,"* Double Cover, inspired
by the book *Prisoners of Our Thoughts* by Dr. Alex Pattakos

Accountability—personal responsibility—tugs at the "brave heart" in all of us. For organizations, it takes on many dimensions of organizational life. As we've learned, it calls on us to courageously challenge what's wrong, to be committed to mission for the long term, and to be that leader that brings the best out in us all: wealth with hard work, knowledge with principle, commerce with morality, science with humanity, pleasure with conscience.

Sometimes the constant need for the human dimension of leadership in our businesses and organizations, as we've learned from some of the stories in this book, gets mistakenly classified like other short-term strategies. "We've spent two years with a focus on people; we need to move on." Unfortunately, and often without too much thought, this happens. Our mindshare for the people, essential to our missions, waxes and wanes. For example, in recent years, we've seen trendy economic and business methodologies take center stage.

One courageous leader who crossed my path taught me a meaningful lesson about the depth of one's sense of personal responsibility and accountability for putting our differences to work for the long term. At the time, issues of people and diversity and inclusion were getting a lot of attention throughout her company. She held the accountability for the overall organizational success. Lots of people were stepping up, putting themselves and their work in the limelight of what had become a popular, visible movement, commanding attention all the way to the top. I saw her gracefully move aside, quietly supporting, allowing plenty of room for each of them to take in the acknowledgment and attention they appeared to be working so hard to garner. One day, I asked her about it. Her message to me was sure and clear: "You see some great things are getting done in the process. We're gaining ground—and when all these people have moved on to other passions, for me, this is a mission." As time went on, I had a chance to see this process unfold. People did move on. The mission survived. Changes, once just dreams, happened.

Susan B. Anthony, a pioneer for putting our differences to work in the nineteenth century, sums up the commitment that comes with the action step of accountability:

> Cautious, careful people, always casting about to preserve their reputation and social standing, never can bring about a reform. Those who are really in earnest must be willing to be anything ... or nothing in the world's estimation—publicly and privately, in season and out,— avow their sympathy with despised and persecuted ideas and bear the consequences.

Whether you are aligning policies, practices, behaviors, actions, and values or opening the way for personal leadership, at the core, it is people who will lead change. People are the innovators, leaders, and high performers. It is the consciousness—and thus accountability—of every person at every level that will help you realize the fastest way to unleash new levels of excellence.

What comes up for me as we have reached the call to action for Step 4 is that the Five Distinctive Qualities of Leadership are the *mirrors* of accountability and personal responsibility needed for putting differences to work. Imagine the *questions* they are asking you as they reflect on your every move through any given day:

How did you incorporate differences into your contribution today?

How did your curiosity help you learn from someone different from you?

In what way did you broaden the notion of open, honest communication with others?

What personal responsibility did you step up to take?

What decisions or actions did you take that demonstrated that you chose mutualism as the final arbiter?

How did everyone benefit from your contribution?

Behavior is the mirror in which everyone shows their image.

—Johann Wolfgang von Goethe

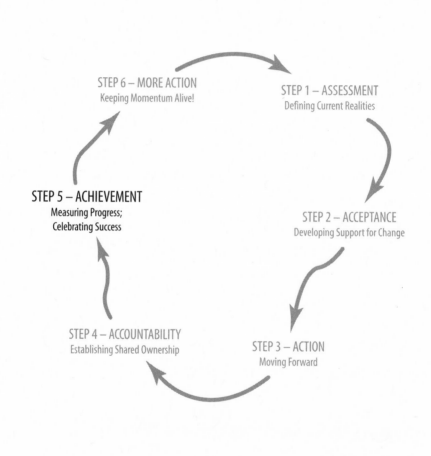

STEP 6 – MORE ACTION
Keeping Momentum Alive!

STEP 1 – ASSESSMENT
Defining Current Realities

STEP 5 – ACHIEVEMENT
Measuring Progress;
Celebrating Success

STEP 2 – ACCEPTANCE
Developing Support for Change

STEP 4 – ACCOUNTABILITY
Establishing Shared Ownership

STEP 3 – ACTION
Moving Forward

> " Here's to the crazy ones, the misfits, the rebels, the troublemakers, the round pegs in the square holes ... the ones who see things differently—they're not fond of rules.... You can quote them, disagree with them, glorify or vilify them, but the only thing you can't do is ignore them because they change things ... they push the human race forward. "

—Steve Jobs
CEO and cofounder, Apple

CHAPTER 8

Step 5—Achievement: Measuring Progress; Celebrating Success

Arriving at the milestone of *achievement*—even a seemingly small one—has its momentary parallels to standing on top of the mountain that took you to a new pinnacle of personal attainment. There is no band playing. It's just you—often exhausted from the climb, perhaps banged up a bit from slipping on the rocks a few times, but elated as you take the magnificent view and yelp inside, "Yes!" If you know this moment, feel blessed. Some leaders, who might do this well at the top of the mountain, struggle seeing, acknowledging, and valuing milestones of progress along the way. For some, it's all or nothing—and all is quickly followed by "What's next?" One leader told me once, "Look, when I get recognized, the people will get recognized."

As you expand your efforts to put differences to work, there are many lessons to apply from the pioneering of human freedoms, justice, and equality that opened the way for us today. They helped us acknowledge our many dimensions of diversity as human beings. The aspirations are ever-changing and evolving as we gain more knowledge, know-how, and experience about the advantages and benefits of working together—solving problems together—pioneering, innovating, and leading together in a world that has become smaller through technology and globalization.

Considerations of diversity and inclusion have been woven into my life and work for many years, not because I went looking for it. Instead, my curiosity and interest made the human dimensions of work and life part of whatever came in front of me. So, as I reflect on what the journey behind us has to offer—even from my small window into it that came from being a leader of people—there are vivid memories of witnessing the *power of one* and the *power of many* achieving greatness. Now it is our turn.

What has become clear to me is that we seldom see our individual leadership contributions as a part of that continuing legacy—our hard work and seemingly small successes, in the name of fundamental fairness, diversity, and inclusion, pass by most of us with never more than a moment's notice. Whether we successfully complete a big event with great influence, successfully lead a significant innovation that emerged out of the strength of the people in our organizations, see statistical reports showing organizational progress in building a diverse global team, or recognize the difference in someone's life we may have touched, the achievements are fleeting. Most often we only recognize there is so much left to do.

As we work to lay a foundation for putting our differences to work at a new time in history—an effort that we recognize is the fastest way to new innovations, new levels of creativity, new opportunities to take the lead, and new pinnacles of achievement to reach—we have to develop a new consciousness about the value of measuring progress and celebrating success. Perhaps there isn't time to linger on every small task we accomplish, but we can at least acknowledge them. Revisit them over and over again to help us see how far we have come. They, in turn, encourage us to start again and give us the will to do more.

The call to all of this generation's leaders—new and seasoned—is to join together to revitalize, refresh, renew our commitment to the people-focused values that reside inside each of us as a first step. If you've mastered this part of leadership, you are to be commended. If you feel that sinking feeling that perhaps you've been neglectful unintentionally, begin again.

In my first management job with IBM, I remember the pressures were many and heavy. I also had two poor performers who were taking an inordinate amount of my time. One day, I walked by the desk of my best employee. She had her head on her desk, exhausted from the long hours we were all working to pull ourselves out of the organizational hole and obviously bewildered. I asked her what was wrong. She said, "I wish I were a problem." All she wanted was a little of my concern and acknowledgment—just a little time—and I was too busy to even notice, too wrapped up in my own overload to perform my basic people leadership responsibilities with my best performer, who never let me down! *Oooh.* As I write, I still remember it painfully. It was a *big* lesson.

Feel fortunate if you work for an organization or in a community that has people-focused values to guide your direction, but if you don't, be a maverick and make your own. It doesn't take a rocket scientist, or an organization, for you to set a few "standards of conduct" for yourself as a leader—standards that include a day-to-day consciousness about appreciating people—caring about them and enjoying the privilege you have to work with them. The Five Distinctive Qualities of Leadership create a framework with which to begin.

Additionally, in the midst of all our busyness, it is easy to overlook or disregard one of the major catalysts for renewing our day-to-day consciousness and commitment for putting our differences to work and living up to our leadership responsibilities to the human beings we lead. It is *reflection*. The echo of the gentle counsel of Carmelite nun Sister Corita Kent says it nicely: "Trying to be good may be to stop running and take time to be quiet and discover who you are and where you have been." The pauses we make don't need to be long. Even a few moments can be powerful in shaping a new level of action and appreciation for others. Leadership at all levels is a privilege, and with privileges come responsibilities.

Nelson Mandela, on the last page of his book *Long Walk to Freedom*, reminds us of the power of reflection on our achievements, role-modeling for us what comes next.

> I have walked the long road to freedom.
> I have tried not to falter; I have made missteps along the way.
> But I have discovered the secret that after climbing a great hill,
> one only finds that there are many more hills to climb.
> I have taken a moment here to rest,
> to steal a view of the glorious vista that surrounds me,
> to look back on the distance I have come.
> But I can rest only for a moment,
> for with freedom come responsibilities,
> and I dare not linger,
> for my long walk is not yet ended.

THE FASTEST WAY IDEAS FOR STEP 5—ACHIEVEMENT

Organizational Snapshot Prompter
Before filling your mind with others' ideas, take a quick organizational snapshot. It will give more meaning to the best practices stories, strategy, and tactical ideas that follow (see the Resources and Studies section).

Achievements come in many forms. What could we learn about our human achievements from the birth of personal leadership in an individual, the discoveries of a global explorer, and an executive who turns progress into a vivid picture of new possibilities and new signs of achievement? I'll let you be the judge as we look at three powerful best practices, along with ideas to prompt your thinking and action.

Best Practice—Corporation and Nonprofit (Partnership)

We always remember the leaders who teach us by their example more than their words. This is a story of one leader who touched my life. I don't know where he is now or recall his last name, but this story is dedicated to his profound influence on many over the years when I've told of his discovery of his personal greatness.

BOB

He was twenty-four years old with a promising future. Then, unexpectedly, life changed. Bob was in a motorcycle accident that left him a paraplegic. We met when he had been in his wheelchair only about eighteen months. He was nominated for a computer programming training program at the Resource Center for the Handicapped (RCH) in Seattle. At the time, I worked for IBM, one of the sponsoring companies, and I was actively involved in this program.

Bob was one of our brightest students, but his growing anguish over his new reality was turning him into an embittered, belligerent, disrespectful noncontributor in the program. The whole class was impacted by his acting out. After exhaustive counseling and coaching efforts, I was given the duty to inform him of his impending expulsion from the program. The moment—and his face—remain vivid in my memory. "You have until Monday, Bob," I told him. "You have until Monday to decide if changing and staying here is worth it to you." He left in a screaming fury.

None of us knew what Monday would bring. I hoped. About five minutes before class started, I looked up and there he was. No words were spoken. We just looked at each other. We both heard in the silence, "Please give me a chance."

Bob went on to graduate number two in his class. He went to work for a major company as a programmer. He was promoted several times the first two years. More importantly, he volunteered his time, going back into the hospitals to become a role model for others. He brought hope to those searching to make sense of the new rules brought about with one of life's paradigm shifts. Soon he was named Washington State Volunteer of the Year.

That year, there was a picture of Bob on the back of the RCH Annual Report. It remains imprinted on my mind. He was climbing the

University of Washington Climbing Rock (I understand he was the first paraplegic to have this achievement). The sweat was pouring down his face, showing the might, passion, and grit that had taken over, reflecting the strength of all he had become. His hands clutched around the rope, pulling energy from within. The caption read, "The biggest engineering feat is that of human will." This is the challenge we all have as leaders—to harness our own human will to change ourselves, so we can lead the way for others.

KEY POINTS: BOB'S STORY

▶ Getting to know people and their differences helps you help others reach inside to bring their best to an organization and the world.

▶ Enabling rich communication makes it possible to help others live up to behavior and actions that foster putting our differences to work; sometimes rich communication is demonstrated without words.

▶ Harnessing our own human will to change is the achievement that makes it possible for us to lead the way for others.

Claude M. Bristol, author of the still-best-selling 1948 book *The Magic of Believing*, put the power of achievement we all have within in perspective when he said, "History is replete with stories of strong-minded, resolutely willed individuals, steadfastly holding to their inner convictions, that have been able to inspire their fellow-man, in the face of tremendous and determined opposition, have literally created out of nothing great businesses ... and new worlds."

Best Practice—Global Citizen

HP was celebrating the tenth anniversary of its professional and technical women's conferences, which evolved from the pioneering spirit and a dream of a few courageous women. At the request of one of my key customers actively involved and one of its sponsors, I was invited to work behind the scenes with the executives and keynote speakers as a producer.

This is how I met Catherine DeVrye. She is the author of numerous books, including *Hope Happens!, Good Service Is Good Business, Japan: An A to Z,* and *Serendipity Road: A Memoir.* She was chosen Australian Executive Woman of the Year in 1993. What I didn't know at the time was that she also had a leadership career with IBM, serving for ten years in

Asia-Pacific; had been the CEO for Junior Achievement Australia; and had a quite remarkable personal story of struggle and achievement. Catherine has not stopped there. She continues to put her mark on the world as a bestselling author, adventurer, and humanitarian. We continue to cheer one another from a distance. She once shared with me a meaningful story about what she had learned as a global citizen, inviting us to see how easily we can make the human connection with others a daily achievement:

CATHERINE DEVRYE

The more I travel, the more I realize that people are the same. There are distinct differences in terms of ways of doing business and cultural sensitivities, but there are more similarities between people than differences. We share similar hopes and fears. Basically, we all want to have the finest possible lifestyle for our families and do our own personal best to gain job satisfaction and enough money to enjoy our leisure. At work, we share the same frustrations of not enough hours in the day, too much bureaucracy, internal politics, computers that break, or mobile phones that are out of range. Even if some of us have never heard of a cell phone, we are still subject to changing conditions in our external environments over which we have no control, whether it be trade sanctions or floods that wipe out an annual crop.

Coming from a country of twenty million Down Under, I've been apprehensive about speaking in India, Korea, Indonesia—even Edinburgh or Fort Collins. Will they have the same sense of humor as audiences in Sydney? Are the issues the same? Will my thoughts be relevant? Inevitably, fears are allayed, in spite of the in-flight magazine being in a totally different language and, perhaps, being served marinated eel for breakfast.

Don't be concerned if you never really understand everything about doing business globally. You probably never will. But it is better to know what you do not know and have an open mind than to think you understand what you really do not. Certainly there are different value systems, and some countries are more spiritualistic than materialistic, but even these goals don't need to be mutually exclusive. Whether it is a toothless smile from an old man at the base of the Great Wall of China or the pearly whites of an eight-year-old in Kenya, I am constantly reminded of the universality of the human race.

As a little girl, my grandfather used to tell me, "A smile is a frown turned upside down." His only travel was when he migrated from Scotland to Canada at the turn of the last century. He would marvel at the changes in today's world, but one thing hasn't changed—smiles are still passports through deserts and visas to all foreign countries.

KEY POINTS: CATHERINE DEVRYE'S STORY

▸ We have our unique differences, but as people across the world, we share similar hopes and fears for our lives; at work, we share many of the same frustrations.

▸ Maintain a curiosity about others differences in culture, business, and society; you will achieve more with an open mind. Do not think you understand what you really do not.

▸ Smiles become a passport for achievement in putting our differences to work.

Best Practice—Corporation

An article in *Fast Company* acknowledges and recognizes J. T. (Ted) Childs Jr., former Vice President of Global Workforce Diversity for IBM, as perhaps the most effective powerful diversity executive on the planet. When you look at his achievements, it would be difficult for anyone to challenge this claim, but to me, it's more personal. Teacher, role model, and mentor by his actions alone better describes my connection to his significant work.

I've only personally seen him a handful of times, and on a few occasions, we've talked, but I've watched him year after year use his innovative mind and trailblazing influence to put differences to work directly tied to business all over the world. No wonder his business, Ted Childs, LLC, has a motto of "Workforce Diversity: The bridge between the workplace and the marketplace."

I met him early in my leadership career. He gave a presentation in a meeting that forever changed my belief in the possibilities of putting differences to work. The most valuable lesson I learned from him was how easy it is to infuse others with courage by your belief in them and by speaking your truth in a way that expresses it.

I received a compelling proposal for IBM to develop, direct, and produce an event to honor the achievements at the Special Olympics that year. My budget was tapped out. I started looking around with my tin cup. No takers. So I called Ted Childs. Actually, I left a few messages in desperation to find money. No response. In retrospect, he was probably giving me a little time to figure this one out for myself. But when I didn't, he called. I don't remember there being even a "hello," but I remember every word he said. "Debbe [said with a tone of belief in me, followed by a stern, commanding moment of truth], do you honestly think IBM is going to fire you for investing in honoring the achievements of some well-deserving Special Olympic athletes? Do it!" No response was needed. I got it!

Over the years, Ted Childs has taught me, and many others, lessons from his amazing capacity to *do* with a flourish what you hear about, read about, and now listen to and watch on the Internet. We talked one morning while he was still at IBM, and he shared this story, which offered a glimpse into the future that we now hold, full of possibilities, signs of progress, and new hope for putting our differences to work:

J. T. (TED) CHILDS

There are signs of people coming together all over the world—gatherings that might not have happened at one time. As an example, I've attended the Leadership Conference for Civil Rights Dinner in Washington, D.C. The Leadership Conference represents a coming together of all of the civil rights organizations—minority, gender, gay/lesbian, aging, and others—under one roof to form an alliance, because they are all fighting for something—fairness and equal treatment for themselves and each other.

We have seen the same kind of energy emerge as IBM's various diversity councils within the company have been formed—people coming together to help us better understand the issues as a company and better understand each other around the world, so we can have the best possible team representing IBM in the marketplace to support our diverse customers.

As we have been working to reinforce the link between our workplace and our marketplace at IBM, we have discovered opportunities to bring people together we had overlooked. For example, we had situations where people tried to buy from us and couldn't: A man from Mexico once called the 800 number and there wasn't anyone on duty that spoke Spanish. He had called to place an order. We had four people who worked in the call center who spoke Spanish, but they weren't on duty. Having someone who speaks Spanish on duty all the time is helping us make connections.

We have also recognized as we are building a global culture of inclusion that it means, no matter who you are at IBM, you will have to work with coworkers and customers who are different from you—black, white, brown, red, or yellow, young or old, gay or straight, male or female, able bodied or physically challenged. People who don't live in your neighborhood. People who don't pray in your church. People who don't come from where you come from. Working here means respecting the diversity we represent.

KEY POINTS: J.T. (TED) CHILDS'S STORY

▶ Sometimes achievement is taking a personal risk to do what you know is right, especially when it benefits everyone.

▶ Putting our differences to work by coming together helps us better understand issues as organizations and better understand each other around the world.

▶ Building a global culture of inclusion means working with people different from you and representing the diversity they represent. There are signs of progress that were once just dreams.

ACHIEVEMENT:
Strategy and Tactical Ideas

Here are three ideas to foster your thinking and action for recognizing progress, measuring and celebrating our efforts, big and small, in putting our differences to work.

▶ **Express your gratitude.** *In Thanks: How the New Science of Gratitude Can Make You Happier,* Robert Emmons shares that two stages of gratitude can be applied to our work in putting differences to work: (1) acknowledging the goodness in what has been achieved and (2) recognizing that the source of this goodness has come from the talents of many. He also helps us understand what the essential components are to expressing gratitude in a meaningful way, using the French expression "je suis reconnaissant," looking closely at the translation in three parts: "(1) 'I recognize' (intellectually), (2) 'I acknowledge' (willingly), and (3) 'I appreciate' (emotionally). Only when all three come together is gratitude complete." Think about how you can express gratitude for the progress you are making in putting our differences to work. Gratitude strengthens the goodness that comes from a diverse, inclusive environment and the inherent joy that comes when we achieve together. It helps us see how far we have come.

▶ **Celebrate in silence.** The measurement of whether we have created a diverse, inclusive environment that puts our differences to work is often understood more by what is seen, felt, sensed, and experienced than by numbers or words. If you have worked or lived in such a welcoming place, no words are particularly necessary—or capable of describing what you know from being in it. Here are a few celebrations to be done in silence: (1) Smile more—it is a way to spread contentment. (2) Take a mental inventory each day of how you contributed to creating a diverse, inclusive organization. This personal ritual will help you stay focused. (3) Send an email to a coworker or a colleague to say you are glad he or she is on the team or to express appreciation of a contribution that has helped everyone work better together. (4) Take one minute regularly to look out and around and feel a sense of gratitude for the people and the community of which you are a part. (5) Think about what you might do to help others cultivate these habits of reflection and action. Success is often a very quiet place inside us with a powerful capability to radiate outward to others. Help it.

▶ **Let results speak for themselves.** Expand your thinking about "business measures" to include measurements that reflect your progress toward your goals for putting our differences to work. For example, if your goals included improving employee satisfaction, instilling the Five Distinctive Qualities of Leadership, and increasing representation at all levels of your organization, post summaries of results to your business record. This might include scores from your employee survey, stories of leaders demonstrating the qualities in action, descriptions of new hires or people promoted, and customer success stories.

ACHIEVEMENT:
A Call to Action

> " Competition is a by-product of productive work, not its goal. A creative man is motivated by the desire to achieve, not by the desire to beat others. "
>
> —Ayn Rand
> Russian American novelist and philosopher

They say there is truth in numbers. So we've commonly measured progress for diversity and inclusion on how many of this *sort* and that *type* we have—how many are on the board of directors, how many are in the markets we serve and the community we want to reach, in the jobs and levels of stature on the organization chart, in the congregation that fills the pews, among the men and women who serve and protect our countries and communities. These are important numbers. They are the benchmarks between our intentions and the results we achieve. They keep us honest to some degree perhaps.

Unfortunately, what these statistics don't measure is change in mindset. Change in belief. Change in attitude. Change in heart. Change in the impact of our actions and behaviors on others. Change in our willingness to be inclusive of everyone—to see each of us as a whole person made up of many dimensions of diversity, including how we think, how we solve problems, what we see in the world around us, the dazzling ideas that we have, and everything that makes us who we are. The numbers are only signs—easily played with and jockeyed around to make us look good in public mirrors, but do they really tell the truth?

As we strive to put our differences to work on many fronts, we face the challenge of holding ourselves to higher standards for recognizing and rewarding achievement that cannot be counted in *sorts* and *types*. We have to develop a keen eye to see successes in the making, especially those visible in people who have become more in the process.

Helen Keller—author, activist, lecturer, the first blind and deaf person to graduate from college, and leadership role model—and her remarkable teacher, Anne Sullivan Macy, demonstrated the power of putting our differences to work for over fifty years. In *Take a Look at Yourself*, a treasured old book now out of print, I read this account of one night when they came together to Denver on a tour. In reading it, you get a real sense about the experience of achievement from two leaders with very different points of view:

> Helen Keller stood on the stage, her fingertips on the violin of a great master, while he played "Ah, Sweet Mystery of Life." She began to sway gently and to keep time with her free hand, as she caught the rhythm; and she turned to the audience, when the sweet mystery was done, to say, with tears in her eyes, "I have found life so beautiful!" Back in the shadows, out of the spotlight, getting none of the applause and wanting none of it, stood Mrs. Macy.

One can imagine the joy in the moment of achievement from both student and teacher. May we discover such moments of achievement in our own work.

Progress leads to achievement;
Achievement inspires dreams;
Dreams give us hope.

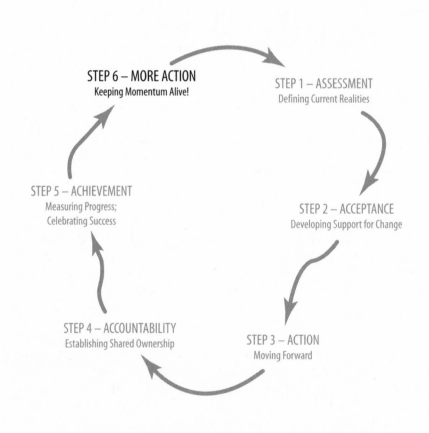

STEP 6 – MORE ACTION
Keeping Momentum Alive!

STEP 1 – ASSESSMENT
Defining Current Realities

STEP 5 – ACHIEVEMENT
Measuring Progress;
Celebrating Success

STEP 2 – ACCEPTANCE
Developing Support for Change

STEP 4 – ACCOUNTABILITY
Establishing Shared Ownership

STEP 3 – ACTION
Moving Forward

CHAPTER 9

Step 6—More Action: Keeping Momentum Alive

Of all six steps that make up the putting our differences to work "perpetual cycle of action," more action is the step that breathes new life into the ongoing journey. Some people tell me they've not made it this far before. My guess is that we all have—we've just not taken time to notice. It is not a destination; it is the gateway to what comes next at any phase of change. It represents the process of reflection, renewal, reenergizing, refocusing, revitalizing, regrouping—and recommitting ourselves and our organizations to what action is needed next. Sometimes, we reach this point after achieving a series of short-term goals. It enables us to step up our momentum for greater change. Other times, we arrive here after several years of hard work and achievement, ready to take on new levels of change. If we are diligent, we wind up here over and over again, each time with the ability to see the journey ahead with a different perspective and a lot of progress to fuel enthusiasm to keep going.

More action is often preceded by what seems a lull, a disruption, an unexpected wind that knocks us over, a pause, a place where we stand still—or at times, we temporarily take a step backward for myriad reasons that we could all recite. This panics the best of us—and if it doesn't, it is often because we are so exhausted by the effort it took to travel this far. While we wait, a fog sometimes seems to settle in. What do we do now? How do we get up for another round? How do we keep from losing momentum?

It seems like an uphill battle with organizational mindshare on other pressures. Perhaps an environment of sameness and separation was easier than putting our differences to work. *Was it, really?* Was it better than what we can accomplish together? There is no going back! The future is always on the road ahead. With patience and a keen awareness, the opening emerges to start anew.

Earlier I introduced Kazuo Inamori, one of Japan's leading entrepreneurs, believers in people, and founder and chairman emeritus of the Kyocera Corporation. He speaks of this moment when he talks about the Kyocera Philosophy: "Every time you take a step forward, the next step will become apparent.

Five Distinctive Qualities of Leadership

1 Makes diversity an organizational priority.

2 Gets to know people and their differences.

3 Enables rich communication.

4 Holds personal responsibility as a core value.

5 Establishes mutualism as the final arbiter.

In this way great things are achieved. Proceed step by step, like an inchworm. This is the way to take up the challenge of great things—not with some extravagant gesture, but with many small steps."

From the moment the Five Distinctive Qualities of Leadership were introduced in Chapter 1, defining what it means to put our differences to work and what distinguishes this new level of thinking and action, the foundation was being laid for building a new generation of conscious organizations led by conscious leaders.

How does a conscious organization operate differently, and why is it relevant to the more action phase? You might be saying, "We are a conscious organization already." If so, great! But I think many organizations that quickly respond in defense often haven't looked close enough to really know. This isn't just about the values on the wall or the public track record of social responsibility or donations and sponsorship for meaningful causes. Consciousness is much more about how you operate and function as a whole organization. The more action phase is frequently when the organization and its leaders at all levels begin to question themselves more objectively. John Renesch, futurist and author of *Getting to the Better Future: A Matter of Conscious Choosing,* offers his insight on what conscious organization means in the context of a people-focused organization:

> The "conscious organization" is not an end-state where every worker has been certified "enlightened" and each and every element of the company, or division or bureau, or agency, or institution is spotlessly cleaned of any residual unconsciousness. The conscious organization

is one which continually examines itself, committed to becoming as conscious as it can. In other words, it has very low tolerance for unconsciousness. It possesses the collective will to be vigilant, the collective commitment to continuous evolution, and the collective courage to act. What I mean by "consciousness" is becoming aware of something and then acting responsibly in light of the new awareness.

It is in the more action phase that we can use our heightened awareness about putting our differences to work and all the values that are wrapped up in it as tools for organizational renewal at a new level. We can look more closely at how our organizational values and behaviors are aligned with practice. We can look at our human frailties with more of a compassionate yet objective look, knowing we are getting better with each day we commit ourselves. John Renesch describes a meaningful example of the kinds of evaluations you do when you've become "conscious" about how you operate with a new commitment to mutualism:

> An organization which holds honesty and integrity high on its list of core ideals, might want to look beyond the mere "misinformation" given by the salesperson and search for where and how this happened. They might question whether or not it was an isolated incident or a mere symptom of a larger more insidious "virus" in the core body of the company.

Once the new level of conscious habits sets in and you're approaching the more action phase, you'll see lots of gaps in rightness in small things that will tug at your new convictions—and as a leader, you are left to grapple with making conscious decisions and sometimes speaking up. The real challenges are the ones that directly affect people's lives—like layoffs, cuts in benefits, outsourcing of jobs, closures, and similar life-changing events. A prime example is the best practice story that Jerrold Tucker related in Chapter 5 about his first day as Chief Learning Officer and the painful lessons that came from straying from the company's values.

Organizations of all kinds have tough decisions to make at times, but conscious leaders and conscious organizations go about them much differently than perhaps a consultant or legal staff might suggest. They also are committed to finding ways to innovate, leading and executing at the highest levels of performance to avoid the human tragedies that we all witnessed in recent years in corporations, our communities, and our governments. Self-examination is best done by the people who make up an organization. One stellar example stays with me from my early leadership career at IBM.

Long before I arrived at IBM and later became a manager, CEO Thomas J. Watson Jr., the founder's son, had started a practice of writing "Management Briefings." His first was written in 1958. They became a tradition, and the whole collection was passed down to each new manager in a navy blue IBM binder in one of the first management schools. In 1988, they gave us all a bound book of these leadership treasures covering thirty years. Today, they continue to be a great source of leadership mentoring for me. As a young leader, receiving them made me feel like I was part of a very special leadership team. Tom Watson's Management Briefings were distinctive and most of them timeless, because he wrote them in personalized plain talk, not corporate speak, as if he was talking with you. I can still almost hear his voice as I read them today. They had a clear purpose: to inform leaders across the company in language you could actually use to talk with your people. Nice touch!

Watson also was famous for incorporating "object lessons" into the briefings. If he observed behavior or heard about actions that were not aligned with our success, he would say so. He would find the lesson in the mistake or bad behavior or insensitive action and help us all learn from it, as a mentor would. Some people joked about the letters, but the day they were released, there was a definite buzz—and we got the messages loud and clear. He also used these letters to instill fundamentals of leadership, restate expectations, and acknowledge great leadership. As the company would reach a time for more action at IBM, one of his letters would prompt leaders again to join him in a collective examination of conscience:

THOMAS J. WATSON JR., MARCH 16, 1961

Many things are responsible for the success of IBM, and we can profit by taking a fresh look at these things once in a while. One of the things my father always tried to impress me with was that the success we want as individuals and as a business is the kind that is built and sustained by the goodwill of other people. None of us wants any other kind of success, even though it might sometimes seem tempting to take a short cut.

Today, organizations of every kind have many technology tools available providing expansive new opportunities and new ways to reexamine, reevaluate, connect, communicate, and collaborate when they reach a place for more action. However it works for you, the point is to *do it*!

What makes the time of more action distinctive is that you and your organization reach it with new knowledge and know-how. The lessons learned, the relationships built, the mistakes made, the victories won all make it possible to take on still another opportunity to innovate with more energy and more expertise. Come along and mark a new beginning by moving out—taking on the challenges of more action. Learn from important success stories, step inside the learning process of putting differences to work during this phase, and explore lessons learned about differences and sameness from a global leader's perspective.

THE FASTEST WAY IDEAS
FOR STEP 6—MORE ACTION

Organizational Snapshot Prompter
Before filling your mind with others' ideas, take a quick organizational snapshot. It will give more meaning to the best practices stories, strategy, and tactical ideas that follow (see the Resources and Studies section).

There has been quite a buzz around James Surowiecki's book for some time, *The Wisdom of Crowds*, which does a fascinating job exploring what is described as a "deceptively simple idea: Large groups of people are smarter than an elite few, no matter how brilliant—better at solving problems, fostering innovation, coming to wise decisions, even predicting the future." What I most appreciate about Surowiecki's book is that it serves as a reawakening about what has been there all along: *people*. In small, medium-sized, and worldwide groups, infuse them with shared vision and an environment of inclusion, and they can do amazing breakthrough work.

Somehow, all this seems familiar. My mind fills with flashbacks of many achievements, past and present. As Mark Twain wryly observed, "The ancients stole all our good ideas." So what's new? For one, as Surowiecki confirms, we have new technology tools with Web 2.0 and beyond that are opening up possibilities at breakneck speed for us to participate and communicate with one another.

We have a chance at this time in history to take all the good we've learned about people—about ourselves—and put all our brilliance to work to generate the innovations we need to solve our most pressing problems. We need to grow and nurture our own brilliance by believing in ourselves and those that work with us. We need to believe enough that they feel empowered to reach inside themselves to discover the potential that exists for greatness, leadership, and contribution.

So, what's the proof point that people have this kind of capability without being considered an expert? Let's look at three very different stories—one putting the spotlight on a leader's experience in reaching a place of more action, one from a leader discovering her wisdom in the time of reflection, and one from a medical doctor and a visionary with a global perspective, helping us all learn as we reach the place of *more action* about what we are capable of doing together through the power of expanding our vision.

Best Practice—Corporation

Jerrold Tucker, the former Assistant Vice President, Learning Solutions, at GTE that I introduced in Chapter 5, told me a story about his team that serves as another powerful validation of the expertise we hold within us at all levels of leadership.

JERROLD TUCKER

As leaders, I think we often have the best intentions when we communicate our visions for the future to people in our organizations. We talk about what we are going to do—trying to paint the picture with words like, we're customer oriented and we're creating shareholder value—never thinking that our trendy business talk really doesn't help the people see their role in fulfilling that vision. We also have a limited view of who can really help us. One time, a talented team of people—administrative clerks, waitresses, housekeepers, curriculum developers, dishwashers, maintenance workers, and instructors—all who worked with me to transform a management development center into a place with a reputation for being one of the premier training centers in the world—helped me see how powerful a vision can be, if you can help every person see how what they do contributes to where you are trying to go.

There were many things about our team that gave us great distinction. It was brimming with ideas and unusual perspectives from many cultures and countries that helped us break through traditional thinking. There were languages spoken from around the world, a gifted poet and musician, abled and disabled side-by-side, some who had overcome great obstacles—each achievers in their own right ready to get involved. A big part of what kept everyone motivated was the time we spent being together—talking, listening, learning from each other, having fun together. The team became as important to each of us as the mission we were on. We discovered great power in our differences, great strength in our sameness—and we put it to work serving customers. As change began to happen everywhere, progress was celebrated. One example was the "find a success story idea" we started. It gave everyone a chance to look for contributions being made by others on the team and write commendations, which we posted on the bulletin board. This small shift helped everyone focus on how much was going right every day.

The great thing about success stories is that they stay with you. If someone asked me today to come up with a lot of good ideas about how to pull a group together, mobilize them, and keep the momentum going, I wouldn't know where to start, but I know who would: the people working there.

KEY POINTS: JERROLD TUCKER'S STORY

▶ Leaders sometimes have a limited view of who can help them most in achieving business and organizational objectives: all the people working there.

▶ A powerful vision can be realized if every person sees how what they do contributes to where you are trying to go. When a team puts their differences to work, it can transform an organization.

▶ Success stories stay with you; they help everyone focus on how much is going right every day as they keep moving forward with more action.

Best Practice—Local Government

Sonia Melara crossed my path some years back in a women's leadership program. Women leaders across private and public sectors came together at Leadership California to put our differences to work in a unique and powerful learning experience. At the time, Sonia was executive director of the City and County of San Francisco Department on the Status of Women. She had a powerful spirit and deep conviction to her mission. I spent a memorable afternoon with her learning about the important work she was involved in on behalf of women. While we were together she also shared this personal story. It will give you an opportunity to step inside a real-life situation to learn how we gain wisdom and expertise by our actions and behavior:

SONIA MELARA

We are such a "melting pot"—and perhaps this is part of the problem of how we view ourselves. While we are a "melting pot" in terms of race, each of us is very unique as individuals, too. Sometimes, I think we forget that each person represents a distinctive part of our individual cultures. We are all different.

When I came here from El Salvador, I came with a belief I owed it to myself to succeed—and the best of all possible worlds here in the United States was where I could do it. In the process of pursuing my goals, other people from my own community would say, "You don't really know about prejudice. You don't really see it." Maybe I did experience it, and for a time I didn't look at it. Over time, I have learned prejudice takes many unexpected forms. For example, when I was nineteen, I applied for the Teacher's Corps to work with farmworkers' children. I was interviewed and later received a letter that the reason they could not employ me was because I was not of Mexican descent and had no experience of the life of the farmworker. I remember thinking, "What? I am a role model." However isolated this example may seem, I think we might all be surprised to find we have common experiences similar to this, where we have been excluded by our own communities, regardless of our race.

I have had many rewarding experiences and achievements. Now, when I am confronted with prejudice, I see it more clearly. At this time in my life, I am in a better place to look at it in the face. I can say, "This is life. These people have limited experiences. This is not about me." I am also grateful that I am in a better place to ask myself, "What am I going to do with this piece of information to make changes?"

To make changes will take a lot of conversation. Diversity has to center around conversation—and the more we have on a daily basis with people who are not like us, the greater chance we have of making the connection between you and me—like we would with someone we wanted to be friends with. This is how you build relationships. You listen. You understand. You learn to be genuine with each other. You figure out together how you can make things different for yourself and others.

KEY POINTS: SONIA MELARA'S STORY

▶ Maybe seeing ourselves as a "melting pot" is part of our problem; in doing so we overlook that each person represents a distinctive part of our individual cultures and everything that makes us individually unique.

▶ Prejudice comes from limited experience of others different than we are. Wisdom to transcend it comes from reflection; changing it comes from more action.

▶ Changing things begins in conversation; together we work to figure out how we can make things different for us all.

Dr. Oguchi Nkwocha, an Igbo visionary from Biafra in southeastern Nigeria, has been instrumental in teaching me about what *more action* really means and what we can do together with the power of a dream. We have worked together for several years through our Global Dialogue Center. We've written together; recorded podcasts together; shared stories and dreams of a better world for business and society—and for the sovereignty of his homeland, Biafra. We've supported one another's passions and important causes. We've put our differences to work.

At the beginning of a new year, a time of renewal and more action for each of us and our businesses and organizations, Oguchi wrote to me about his perspective on the power of vision in propelling people to put their differences to work. He helped me see a familiar story from the perspective of a global citizen—and now I share it with you as you consider the idea of more action.

OGUCHI NKWOCHA, M.D.

We can build new dreams and once again be renewed by a vision that came true in the last century:

On May 25, 1961, President John F. Kennedy articulated a powerful vision and described this dream in his special message before a joint session of Congress on the "Urgent National Needs" of the United States. It was a vision that proves the power of our dreams put into action: "I believe that this nation should commit itself to achieving the goal, before this decade is out, of landing a man on the moon and returning him safely to the Earth."

On July 24, 1969, when *Apollo 11* returned with its crew safely to Earth, following its earlier launch on July 16, 1969, and subsequent successful landing at the Sea of Tranquility on the Moon on July 20, 1969, that dream was fully manifested.

It is important to note that in 1961, this was a truly "Impossible Dream."

Today's space scientists and technologists say what President Kennedy envisioned back then could only have been accomplished with today's knowledge and technology—that is, only with the facilities of forty years later. Stated a different way, Kennedy's dream had snatched from a time fifty years in the future to produce a result in 1969.

Take a moment to consider the clarity and precision of Kennedy's dream. In just one sentence with thirty-one words—two or three lines—he articulated and claimed the goal for the nation and its people:

Who: Our nation

What: Commit to achieve a goal

The goal:

* Land a man on the moon
* Return him to earth
* Return him safely
* Before the decade is out

Results: Immeasurable results came from one sentence and thirty-one words.

Together, through the efforts of all the people involved, we proved that a dream today can pluck from the tree of time desirable fruits which perhaps are meant for a future season; some are not presently available. This is an example of accomplishing the impossible. Yes, it can be done! We proved it.

Why not do the same kind of dreaming for our businesses and organizations, our cities, our nations, and the world?

KEY POINTS: OGUCHI NKWOCHA'S STORY

▶ A vision doesn't have to be long, have an operating model, or be possible; it needs the belief of the leader articulating it.

▶ People putting their differences to work can do the impossible, if the dream is big enough—we proved it.

▶ Lessons from past successes can inspire new visions today as we work to find new paths and keep the momentum alive.

MORE ACTION:
Strategy and Tactical Ideas

Here are three ideas to foster your thinking and action as you consider the important step of more action. Try them to help apply what you've learned and keep momentum alive by engaging people, expanding the conversation, and revitalizing your vision.

▶ **Build a new energy source team.** Put a cross-functional team together to figure out what to do to mobilize a more action effort that will be a catalyst for the next phase of putting differences to work. Begin with a few key questions—agree on the specifics. Then, empower them to go to work. Three sample questions are (1) What's going well to support putting our differences to work and living the Five Distinctive Qualities of Leadership, and what isn't? (2) What do we need to do to revitalize personal involvement and commitment? (3) How would you creatively go about it?

▶ **Start a new conversation.** You can never communicate enough. Conversation is the means by which we build understanding, acceptance, and ownership. Even if you have used some form of dialogue previously, do it again. Change the setting. Change your approach. Change the questions. Taking your work to a new level is not about starting over and finding some new definition or labels for the cause. It is about coming back to the truths and goodness that reside in putting differences to work and exploring new revelations that have emerged, seeing everything with new eyes— coming back again and again to people, places, and situations with fresh perspectives to help us take another bold step forward. Three resources: (1) my own *Diversity Breakthrough! Action Dialogues: Meaningful Conversations to Accelerate Change*—learn more at www.diversitybreakthrough.com; (2) *Working Together: Putting Differences to Work to Innovate, Influence and Win*, another work of mine detailed at www.globaldialoguecenter.com/workingtogether; (3) *Dialogue: Rediscover the Transforming Power of Conversation* by Linda Ellinor and Glenna Gerard.

▶ **Refresh your approach; create a revitalized vision.** Consider how you can take your efforts toward putting differences to a whole new level. Articulate a big dream in a way that everyone can see it. Take on the challenge of reframing the mission in your own words. Make it real and relevant to everyone around you. As you formulate your plans for more action in creating a diverse, inclusive environment in other key areas of influence, don't forget to translate your priorities into individual actions for everyone in the organization so that they can see their important roles. You might even invite a few people to put their differences to work with you to explore ideas about what will work. The three stories in this chapter affirm that the people have the answers, conversation accelerates reaching the next level of understanding and ownership, and a leader with a powerful vision can inspire a dream that everyone will want to be part of as you take putting our differences to work to a new level.

MORE ACTION:
A Call to Action

"Vision is perhaps our greatest strength. It has kept us alive to the power and continuity of thought through the centuries; it makes us peer into the future and lends shape to the unknown."

> —Li Ka-shing
> Chairman, Cheung Kong Holdings
> and Hutchison Whampoa Limited,
> and philanthropist

The quest for putting our differences to work continues—and there is much left to do. It is easy to think that perhaps your relatively small contributions couldn't possibly matter, but change will come from the efforts of millions of leaders across all industries and sectors doing their part. It will come from a change in the collective consciousness of every leader and all people—and we can move to a new level of fundamental fairness, equality, and inclusion by starting with small changes within ourselves as individuals.

In the best-selling book by Claude Bristol entitled *The Magic of Believing* that I mentioned earlier, he speaks about the power of *belief*—the kind of belief that can change a mindset, generate innovations, create new wealth, and achieve new levels of leadership and high performance in marketplaces, workplaces, communities, and our world. One analogy he uses demonstrates the connection between planting a garden and the power behind more action:

> Once the soil is prepared and the tiny seeds are placed in it, it is but a short time when they put forth roots, and sprouts begin to appear. The moment they start upward through the soil in search of light, sunshine and moisture, obstacles mean nothing to them. They push aside small stones or bits of wood, and if they can't do it, they'll extend themselves and grow around them. They are determined to emerge from the ground.

We have planted the seeds. When you have reached the more action phase, the sprouts have made their way through the rockiest soil—and you can see them reaching up and bearing fruit. Now, it is up to us to keep the momentum alive by cultivating a new era where we work together with the intention and conviction to make mutualism a final arbiter of all we do. We need to remain attentive to changing needs, giving them our conscious attention and actions. We are the force that gives life to new ideas and a very different world than we know today.

PART 3

Ever-Expanding Possibilities

" I have climbed several higher mountains... without guide or path, and have found... it takes only more time and patience commonly than to travel the smoothest highway. "

—Henry David Thoreau
Essayist, poet, and philosopher

rriving here, I am again reminded where we started in Part 1. It began by pointing out that there are many parallels between climbing a mountain and the experience of raising one's level of leadership awareness, knowledge, and know-how. We established a goal for this journey to connect you with some of the secrets of reaping the benefits of diversity that reside in people, the benefits that work as a powerful catalyst to accelerate innovation and increased productivity—the kind that inspires a sense of shared achievement by everyone. We've learned that mastering the art of putting our differences to work is a road with many curves, rocky passages, tiny details, and human considerations sometimes hidden behind what is obvious. More importantly, this journey demands that we sharpen our leadership skills by developing a whole new set of qualities that put conscious intention first in all our decisions and actions.

Now, we stop here to begin Part 3 at what I would liken to the experience of reaching a summit on a climb. Nelson Mandela described the wonder of the arrival at such a place, high atop a long and winding journey of growth, in the quote I shared in Chapter 8: "I have taken a moment here to rest, to steal a view of the glorious vista that surrounds me, to look back on the distance I have come."

A summit, for our purposes, is a place to take stock of lessons learned, as well as a place to look out at the panoramic view into the distance; to see, to appreciate, and to use our minds with a new sense of openness about the expanding possibilities for putting our differences to work. These new prospects are emerging all around us in plain sight. Instead of being in the spotlight or part of a flashy headline, more often they are just quietly taking place, opening the way in directions we might not have imagined, changing our consciousness one action at a time, revising the map of how we might work and live together in the future.

The details of the wide-ranging view might not have been noticed, or even cared about, in the same way before having this time to think and question for yourself. Now, after thoughtful consideration of the many points of view in the previous chapters, we are zooming in on a few places in the vast landscape, to look closely at what can be learned, applied, and added to your own collection of discoveries.

To help, I invited futurist Joel Barker to partner with me to share what we've learned, independently and collectively, for over a decade. We've been exploring in parallel from different vantage points to identify the connection between innovation and diversity. We have been experimenting to see how it works in practice. In Chapter 10, "Innovation at the Verge of Differences," Joel affirms with highlights from his research why it is essential for all of us to learn to deal with diversity at all levels—in the boardroom; in the organization; in the field; in the marketplace; in our communities, and in the world. In Chapter 11, "Collaboration at the Verge of Differences," I share our story of meeting at the verge of our own differences and the practical experiment that ensued, highlighting the trials that put our convictions to the test.

I've also invited a small diverse group of innovative "pioneers of practice" to share their stories. Together, we've worked to create a wide-angle view that takes in a unique sampling of experimental efforts to put differences to work. In each case, the individuals stepped into unknown situations to explore what would happen. The results led to the discovery of the power of diversity and something bigger at work than any one person. Each effort, seemingly simple at first glance, holds its own mystery and marvel that could easily be applied to the needs of the most challenging issues we face. Every person involved blended their intellect and experiences to make contributions with distinction—to teach us something. What is shared in common, across the diverse nature of these uncomplicated circumstances, mirrors to all of us the promise of what is possible when we work together for the good of all.

Across the differences represented—explorers of new ideas, trailblazers leaving new footprints on human connection in a corporation or an entrepreneurial venture turned invitation to the world, and a group of uncommon women enriching life itself by showing up—indelible marks have been left on the uncharted territory that landed on their paths. The lessons learned have created the gift I hope you'll take away.

CHAPTER 10

Innovation at the Verge of Differences

by Joel A. Barker

My discovery of the importance of verges for twenty-first-century innovation started with a short article in *Science News*, on August 9, 1997, followed by an extended article in *Discover* magazine in December of that year. The essence of those articles was this: Much to the surprise of some scientists, very significant and radical biological innovation occurs farthest away from the heat of competition. In particular, it occurs where two ecosystems meet, at the edge or *verge*. (The ecological term for verge is *ecotone*.)

I adopted the term *verge* and define it the same way Daniel Boorstin does: *where something and something different meet*. The importance of this definition is that it works both for biological examples and human cultural and technological examples.

The information about innovation at the verge fascinated me, because it flew in the face of the "survival of the fittest" paradigm. According to this view, it is intense competition that drives biological innovation. Yet here was research that had identified another equally rich territory where the innovations were far more radical and risky.

To test the thesis, I did a simple thought experiment: if I were in the midst of intense competition, what kind of adaptations or innovations might I try?

Answer: only those that didn't put me immediately at risk to being eaten—in short, incremental innovations that could fail but not get me killed.

But, if I were in an area where there was far less competition—out at the edge of my ecosystem, for instance—I might be a lot more willing to test more radical innovations, because if I failed, I failed in secret, with minimum risk. No one would be noticing. As I considered all this, I also saw a paradigm "thing" going on here. New paradigms predominantly come from people outside the field. It wasn't the vacuum tube manufacturers that came up with transistors, for example. Quoting from my paradigm film: "If you want to find the new paradigms that are developing in your field, you must look beyond the center to the fringes, because almost always, the new rules are written at the edge. That's where Xerox started. That's where the women's movement started. All of them begin at the edge."

Almost always, the new rules are written at the edge.

When I reviewed my paradigm examples, I found that, indeed, most of the time, it was someone from one field coming up with the revolutionary idea for another field.

Then I thought about the large verges in nature: where the ocean meets the shore; where the land meets the sky. And sure enough, some of the most important innovations in biological history occurred at these verges. Water-breathing animals looked up and out at dry land and saw unique opportunities. So they began a series of radical adaptations (that's innovation, isn't it?) that allowed them to breathe air instead of water and then walk instead of swim. Land animals were born. A similar radical set of innovations led to flight. Insects, birds, bats all solved the problems of vertical mobility in different ways, using very different kinds of flight innovation. But they were successful in moving from the ground to the sky.

As if to complete the circle, land animals looked back to the seas filled with opportunities that were only available to them if they could radically adapt and biologically innovate to live full-time in the oceans. And so seals and walruses and orcas and whales resulted from those adaptations.

Each adaptation represented innovation at the verge. It was the opportunity available on the "other side" that triggered the innovation. And the results changed the world again and again.

Then the question became: if it's true for Mother Nature, is it true for human innovation? The more I looked, the more examples I found of humans innovating new tools, new social inventions, even new religions at the verge. After several years of research, I now believe that this "verge-uous" territory is where the great ideas of the twenty-first century are going to come from. And those organizations that know where this territory is have a great advantage over those that don't.

Before I illustrate this territory, I need to offer a caveat. When I talk about a verge, I am emphasizing the meeting of differences. There can be little differences and big differences. I will focus on big differences, surprising differences, "I can't believe it" differences. Most organizations are pretty good at combining little differences. They are lousy at the big ones.

Let me give you five examples to illustrate the power of innovation at the verge.

Ink Jet Housing

Take an ink jet printer. Enlarge its nozzle until it can squirt out liquid concrete. Build a framework large enough so that it can trace the floor plan of a house in real-life dimensions. Have it go back and forth squeezing out concrete like toothpaste, each time raising up to heighten the walls. In forty-eight to seventy-two hours, you have "printed" a house.

This work is being done at the University of Southern California by Bethrokh Khoshnevis at the School of Engineering. It is innovation at the verge. The verge is between house construction, ink jet printer technology, and concrete technology. The result is a potential radical innovation which could change the housing industry around the world. Remember, I said I focus on big differences. I think this meets that criterion.

Gift Wrap and Paper Bags

The ink jet house printer is very sophisticated technology. But innovation at the verge can be very simple and equally effective. For example, when gift wrap and plain paper bags meet at the verge, what have you got? Gift bags! Completely obvious once they were created, but it took a long time to get there.

What is the advantage of a gift bag? As a man not very good at gift wrapping, I can tell you ease of use. And that's worth a lot to me. For the manufacturer, huge profit margins. Notice that this verge-uous innovation wasn't complex or tricky. It was simply the result of seeing the combination of two very different things.

Debbe and Sally

As Debbe Kennedy has mentioned in the book, we've known one another for many years. I've known her partner, Sally Green, for about the same time. When Debbe explained how she and a graphic artist had formed a company for leadership solutions, I was impressed and thought it was a paradigm shift. Now I know it is also innovation at the verge. By bringing together top-notch leadership consulting and top-flight graphic arts, the two of them have created a monopoly advantage that is very difficult to beat.

Think about two proposals, one from Debbe and Sally, one from a good leadership consulting group. Theirs has been prepared using Word and PowerPoint and it is clear and clean. But the proposal from Debbe and Sally is not only clear and clean; it is also *beautiful*. It is graphically powerful. It has suggestions for graphic icons that the client could use to launch the new leadership program. It has a set of colors that coordinate perfectly and speak to deep considerations about how to visually present the ideas that Debbe and Sally have developed over the years.

Both proposals sit side by side on the CEO's desk. Which would you pick up first? The leadership consultancy combined with powerful custom graphic arts? A tough-to-beat innovation at the verge.

The Toyota Prius

Toyota has created a highly profitable, "green" vehicle by utilizing innovation at the verge. It combined three things: gasoline engine technology, big electric motor and battery technology, and computer controls that mediate how the other two technologies interoperate.

The verge created the opportunity to combine two very different systems—gasoline power and electric power—into a package that creates substantial energy savings. By adding very sophisticated computer controls, the Prius drives like almost any car. And, at least in the first decade of the twenty-first century, there have been no internal combustion engine technologies that could have delivered what the Prius system does in terms of energy consumption, low pollution, and ease of use.

The Cell Phone

Anyone who is carrying a cell phone is carrying one of the greatest innovations at the verge. Remember when they were only used for calling people? And then someone said, "Hey, let's see if we can put a camera in the phone!" Just think about that for a minute: a device used by your ear to hear sound and your voice to send sound is going to add picture taking and sending. Clearly the intersection of differences. Of course, that's all ancient news now as more and more verge-uous features are being added to cell phones almost monthly. In a very real sense, the cell phone is almost a "universal" verge.

Debbe and I have found over a hundred examples of innovation at the verge. When I speak on this topic, audience members come up afterward to share their own stories of innovation at the verge.

APPROACHING THE VERGE TERRITORIES

As I assembled all the examples we've found, I saw three patterns of verge innovation that help me understand how the process unfolds:

▶ **Pattern 1: The "Over There" Approach.** For instance, the inkjet housing system takes inkjet technology and brings it to the house construction territory. Inkjet technology wasn't improved with housing technology. Housing technology was improved with inkjet technology. The inkjet researchers are applying their technology to the housing territory to create a high value, monopoly advantage in house construction.

▶ **Pattern 2: The "Bring It Back" Approach.** The Prius example is exactly the opposite. Toyota went to the big electric motor and battery people and took their technology back to the auto industry territory. But, by combining both technologies, Toyota created a monopoly advantage in the auto industry territory and are dominating the hybrid market.

▶ **Pattern 3: The "New Territory" Approach.** This approach creates a brand-new territory that did not exist before by combining key ideas. Federal Express is an "innovation at the verge" organization. Fred Smith saw an emerging market in the movement of small, high-value items (lots of computer stuff in the 1970s, for instance) that were mission-critical yet too expensive to stockpile. He correctly recognized that by combining small jet planes with local trucks in one smooth logistical chain, he could move those expensive little items overnight at a nifty profit. This innovative delivery system and the territory it created didn't exist until Smith built Fed Ex.

WINNERS AND LOSERS

One more thing about innovation at the verge: while it would be great if all verge innovations were mutualistic, that isn't the way it works. For instance, with the Prius, Toyota and the electric motor suppliers have a mutualistic relationship—both benefit. But for other automakers, the Prius represents a new area of competition with Toyota already dominating it. Not good for them.

With Federal Express, it was mutualistic for everyone until UPS and the U.S. Post Office decided they wanted a piece of the action. But until then, it was only winners: Fed Ex; customers; small-jet builders; truck builders and computer support systems, employees. They all gained and no one lost.

In my video *Wealth, Innovation and Diversity*, I point out that "at the intersection of differences lies the opportunity for innovation."

As a leader who understands the importance of a constant stream of new ideas, I see a huge opportunity for continual innovation at the verge. Your challenge is to take the time to walk away from the heat of competition and, on a regular basis, go to the edge of your territory and scan the horizon, looking for surprising combinations of very different elements.

You should regularly meet with the organizations with which you share a verge, even if it seems trivial or insignificant. Your job: to see if there are opportunities to combine talents, techniques, and technologies in a new way. If you don't make this a scheduled activity, it won't happen. The day-to-day competition will eat up all of your time. You must take the time to go exploring.

As a good friend of mine, architect Jerry Allan, said more than twenty years ago, "The great ideas of the twenty-first century are going to be combinations of the great single ideas of the twentieth century." Debbe has given you wonderful instructions in this book on how to become more innovative at every level in your organization. Innovation at the verge identifies for you a mostly untouched territory worthy of exploring to utilize her instructions.

KEY POINTS: INNOVATION AT THE VERGE
OF DIFFERENCES *FROM JOEL A. BARKER*

▶ The best ideas at the verge are usually the most wacky or even weird on first examination. Don't be afraid of goofy combinations.

▶ By listening to "the outsider" and hearing how they see the verge innovation, you will often be able to expand the application of the new idea.

▶ Without diversity, there can be no verges. Celebrate the differences. Enlarge the differences. It creates more options for innovation.

Note: See the Resources and Studies section for information on Joel Barker's films, books, and tools.

The best ideas at the verge are usually the most wacky or even weird on first examination. Don't be afraid of goofy combinations.

By listening to "the outsider" and hearing how they see the verge innovation, you will often be able to expand the application of the new idea.

Without diversity, there can be no verges. Celebrate the differences. Enlarge the differences. It creates more options for innovation.

—Joel Barker

Innovation at the Verge of Differences

Working at the verge of differences calls for flexible, fluid partnership arrangements, so innovations don't get bogged down in unnecessary complexities that can stall the creative process. Be willing to let go to find solutions to problems that arise.

Innovation at the verge is enabled and enhanced by everyone applying the five distinctive leadership qualities: diversity is a partnership priority; know and value each other's differences; enable rich communication; personal responsibility is a shared core value; mutualism is the final arbiter for decisions.

Mutualism requires a change in mindset and a partnership conviction that everyone benefits and no one is harmed.

—Debbe Kennedy

Innovation at the Verge of Differences:
Joel Barker and Debbe Kennedy Learnings

CHAPTER 11

Collaborating at the Verge of Differences

Have you ever thought about how opposites work well paired together? When it comes to taste, as an example, sweet and salty is a great combination; or consider the pairing of fruit and savory meats in French cooking, or spicy Thai peanut sauce served with cool cucumber. When it comes to color, one goes to the opposite side of the color wheel to find the color that is most complementary, like blue and orange. When it comes to great collaboration, think about the depth of coverage that comes in pairing men and women, an academic with a practitioner, or a left-brain thinker with a right-brain thinker. Rumi, the thirteenth-century Persian poet, saw the great potential in the meeting of opposite ideas when he said, "Beyond the ideas of right-doing and wrong-doing there is a field. I'll meet you there." Joel Barker, the futurist who popularized the concept of paradigm shifts, has been looking for Rumi's field. He thinks he has found it, but if he is right, it is not a field but the intersection between fields that are different from one another. As described in the previous chapter, he uses the term *verge* to describe this kind of intersection. He believes that the verge will be this century's most important territory for innovation.

Joel introduced me to his discovery of the concept of innovation at the verge of differences a few years back. Not uncommon when any of us hears a new idea for the first time, I remember having to consciously work to grasp this new thinking he shared with me. The idea of innovation at the verge changed the rules. My understanding of opposites helped me begin to see what Joel had discovered. I soon realized all opposites represented differences, but all differences aren't necessarily opposites. Joel challenged me to look for examples of innovation that were created as the result of differences meeting at the verge. I found the exercise to be a kind of mind puzzle, creating a whole new way of seeing innovation. I developed a simple drawing to help me practice. I'd identify an innovation, working backward to see the differences that came together to create the new combination.

Let me share an example I created early on related to the far-reaching possibilities that emerged when Microsoft acquired Placeware in 2003, the first commercial Web-conferencing product. Taking virtual meetings to a new level, this merger resulted in the introduction of Web-based collaboration called Microsoft Office Live Meeting®. It made it possible for businesses, big and small, to benefit. I was one of them. With a continuous stream of

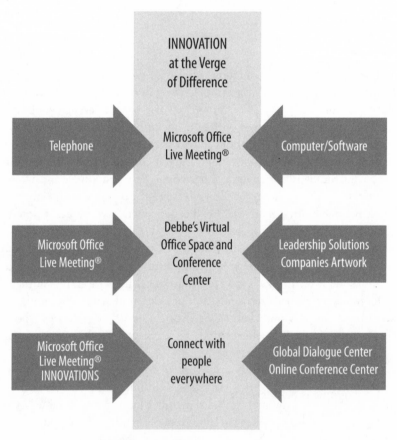

Innovation at the Verge of Difference:
Microsoft Office Live Meeting® Example

other Web 2.0 technologies that have enhanced the initial innovation, it has inspired me to recognize other verges of opportunity. In my own work, I recognized that by combining Live Meeting with one of our organization's hallmarks of success, artwork, I could create a whole new Web-based presence for our company, as well as a distinctive means of conducting business virtually. I innovated at the verge by using Live Meeting and combining it with a kind of art gallery to create a unique virtual meeting space. It turned the look of a Web-based platform into my own branded "virtual office space" to meet and welcome my customers and colleagues (see the Innovation at the Verge of Difference illustration). I've used it as a primary place of business for several years with great success. We used the same technique to transform the experience of attending a webinar at our Global Dialogue Center Conference Center. In 2007, new features were added, including VoIP (Voice over Internet Protocol), video cam, and an array of additional interactive, collaborative, and organizational enhancements. I remember our "maiden voyage" with forty pioneers of virtual space from eleven countries. By simply throwing on a headset and logging on, we were together. Integrating these innovations at the verge into our day-to-day practice has given us a distinctive edge and what Joel calls a "monopoly advantage" in our business.

The concept of innovation at the verge of differences has been a rich part of the collaboration Joel and I have shared. Joel has led the way with research, study, and discovery of the new paradigm. My role has been focusing on how innovation at the verge fundamentally changes the rules of how people operate when they meet, explore, and work in mutualistic collaboration at the verge of their differences. For us, this work has become a practical experiment for us. We've worked independently from our unique perspectives and let out a yelp when we found something exciting in our exploration. The other has always come running to see and support a new find. What has been the most meaningful part is when we go exploring in each other's field of discovery. Joel invites me to journey with him in a territory of his research and study often foreign to me, and in turn, I've done the same for him. Then, we have intentionally worked to put our learning into practice to test how innovation at the verge works in real life. This pattern of research, study, and mutualistic practice has characterized our uncommon collaboration for many years.

One example is demonstrated in the following story of how the experiment happened when we met at the verge. You'll see through its trials and tests what it means to put the Five Distinctive Qualities of Leadership into practice within a collaborative partnership with a key focus on mutualism being the final arbiter of all actions and decisions.

BARKER-KENNEDY EXPERIMENT

Imagination is more important than knowledge. For knowledge is limited to all we now know and understand, while imagination embraces the entire world, and all there ever will be to know and understand.

—Albert Einstein

As a backdrop to the story of our "mutualism experiment," several realizations surfaced in the last couple of years about Joel's and my collaborative work. They surprised both of us. In the fury of curiosity, imagination, and our perpetual drive toward the next idea, they were unnoticed until we began working on Joel's discovery of the vast field of opportunity for innovation that resides at the verge of differences.

The first realization is that we've only met face to face ten times or less in all these years. Most of our collaborative work has been achieved virtually, and it started long before the notion of "virtual" was a mainstream idea for conducting business. Our first communication was via fax. In the early years, we dreamed of distant futures and how technology would make so many things possible. I remember Joel encouraging me to keep going when we worked for two long weeks to launch our company's first website in the early 1990s. In what seems a blink of the eye, Joel and I began working comfortably in virtual space with expanding use of Web 2.0 technologies several years ago. We've laughed a few times about it being a "dream come true" from explorations of ideas years before, marveling at how far we've come and the power of vision that brought us here.

The second realization was recognizing that the two of us represented differences that operated at the verge. Everything about us is different. Across all the dimensions of diversity, we realized we were indeed a diverse, unconventional duo, working in uncommon ways. This seemed to energize our explorations of innovation and diversity, prompting us to pay closer attention and look for new verges where we can put our differences to work. Joel's new film, *Innovation at the Verge*, and this book are two positive outcomes.

It was shortly after the turn of the twenty-first century that we began our mutualism experiment. It started following the launch of Joel's *Wealth, Innovation and Diversity* video. We had worked collaboratively on the film and workshop, putting the differences of our teams and partners to work to create a breakthrough product with a whole new business-focused message about the connection of diversity and innovation.

One of the secrets of our collaborations has been always keeping things simple and uncomplicated. This experiment was no different. We committed to consciously use the principle Joel introduced in *Wealth, Innovation and Diversity*, "Everyone benefits and no one is harmed," in both our subsequent work with the film and all future opportunities. We agreed it would require practice as well as ongoing coaching to instill this principle into our mindsets and the mindset of all who worked with us. We figured by starting with this simple goal, our conscious practice would have a rippling influence on how we operated in any project, collectively or independently. We were right. When you change your consciousness through practice, you develop skills that soon become a habit. On reflection, it is easy to see that the "research and development" for the Five Distinctive Qualities of Leadership were initially tried, tested, refined, and proven in the years of practice with our work and independently in our own businesses, working with clients.

We also learned it is not easy to change everyone's thinking at the same time or to expect that changes are automatic. We found it hard work to think of the implications of one's decisions and actions that met the standard of "Everyone benefits and no one is harmed." This is especially true because most of us are so well trained to look out for our own interests first. So a key learning was that installing and instilling this principle as a quality of leadership takes practice.

Two stories capture the challenges and the crossroads that came up during our experiment working at the verge of differences. Each put our convictions to the test.

The Five Distinctive Qualities Put to the Test

One big lesson was realizing that mutualism isn't just a one-time decision you make at the beginning of a collaborative adventure.

The *Wealth, Innovation and Diversity* video workshop had many fingerprints on it. We worked together to decide how all the various partners would benefit based on their contributions. Everyone agreed to the financial and production model, and a simple agreement was drawn up. It was mutualistic.

Several years after its launch, advances in technology offering more efficient and effective ways to produce the product made our original decisions outdated and obsolete. The result of this change had a quite significant (and negative) financial impact on me. It was an unintentional and unforeseen consequence of upgrading the product that none of us had anticipated. The simple agreement between us didn't really include any provisions to remedy a change in how we produced and marketed the product. The situation put our convictions to the test. All the other partners stood at a crossroads, because changing the arrangements for them meant sharing with me, when there was no contractual obligation to do so. I knew this. I will never forget when Joel wrote me to say that the partners had agreed to revise our financial agreement based on what was right to do with *mutualism as the final arbiter.*

This experience is a poignant example that put all five of the distinctive leadership qualities to the test. We consciously brought a diverse team of innovators together to be drivers of our success. We used everyone's talent, including global know-how, marketplace understanding, and creative thinking to improve and perfect the *Wealth, Innovation and Diversity* product through advances in technology. When the positive changes resulted in negative implications to one of the partners, we had a built a foundation of rich communication, which enabled the problem to be easily raised. All of the partners called upon their own sense of personal responsibility to do what they believed was right to do, when the changes had inadvertently impacted one of the partners. Then they stepped up to live up to our collective commitment to *everyone benefits and no one is harmed.* I learned that mutualism is about character; doing what's right to do, even when you don't have to do it.

Mutualism the Fast and Flexible Way

The second big lesson was recognizing that mutualism doesn't necessarily mean that everyone is all intertwined, operating as one cohesive unit or merging in order to innovate. We've learned that this isn't always the fastest way to innovation, leadership, and high performance.

Traditional teamwork, committees, and collaboration have become synonymous with consensus and interdependence. Joel and I have learned in our experiment that working at the verge of differences often calls for a more flexible and fluid arrangement among partners, so innovations don't get unintentionally bogged down by the weight of the collaboration itself or in complexities and struggles that are usurping time, energy, and the flow of progress.

We found ourselves faced with this exact situation a while back. Joel and I were working together on an innovative project, having great fun and forging new ground, but we landed at an impasse that was adding layers of complexity neither of us wanted to take on. Again, calling upon the openness for ongoing rich communication we had developed, our sense of personal responsibility to each other, and our commitment to mutualism, we resolved the situation. What did we do? Like a well-choreographed dance, we moved away, let go, separated from the unforeseen struggle, and returned to our work independently on the project with the promise we would meet at the verge again when the resolution revealed itself or a better idea emerged. It did. This is how *Putting Our Differences to Work* and Joel's new film *Innovation at the Verge* took flight in record time and with ease.

Whatever is flexible and flowing will tend to grow.

—Lao Tzu

KEY POINTS: COLLABORATING
AT THE VERGE OF DIFFERENCES

▶ Working at the verge of differences calls for flexible and fluid partnership arrangements, so that innovations don't get bogged down in unnecessary complexities that can stall the creative process. Be willing to let go to find solutions to problems that arise.

▶ Innovation at the verge is enabled and enhanced by the Five Distinctive Qualities of Leadership being honored by everyone in the partnership:

• Make diversity a partnership priority.

• Get to know people and their differences.

• Enable rich communication

• Hold a sense of personal responsibility as a core value.

• Establish mutualism as the final arbiter.

▶ Mutualism is a value that requires a change in mindset and conviction by everyone that ensures everyone benefits and no one is harmed by your decisions and actions.

> "Our imagination is the only limit to
> what we can hope to have in the future."
>
> —Charles F. Kettering
> Engineer and inventor

CHAPTER 12

The Power of the Virtual Gathering Place

We should all be so grateful for the advent of enterprises like MySpace, You-Tube, Skype, SecondLife, and Facebook. They have opened new frontiers for putting our differences to work beyond our wildest imaginations—and at lightning speed, with all the usual fits and starts and controversy that innovations inherently bring. These innovations have democratized communication, breaking down barriers across the world that have made it possible to get to know one another and learn about our differences across generations, cultures, and distance. Even the most Internet-averse have heard and read at least the buzz about these Internet icons, and they have been a catalyst for all kinds of new partnerships and collaborations, as well as an opener of the floodgate to get people engaged in very different ways of communicating with one another.

I remember the first time I held a Skypecast, one of the options on Skype, an innovative software that allows you to make phone calls through your computer to any Skype member worldwide and with many other features and tools (www.skype.com). My Skypecast was a one-hour, self-generated dialogue at a designated time. I posted a brief ad about the event that shows in the Skypecast schedule. I chose the option of it being an open invitation versus a private session. When I logged on, in an instant, nearly fifty people showed up from over ten countries that I could discern, including Greece, China, the United Kingdom, Australia, Romania, India, Canada, South Africa, and the United States. They came to explore ideas about "being good neighbors." It was primitive and awkward at first, because we were all trying something new. The technology was still in beta test, and I would say all of us were, too. Some people talked. Some listened, but you couldn't help but feel our curiosity about each other and the thrill for many of being heard. There were shy voices, provocative opinions, people wanting to tell you about their culture and view of the world. Together, we got a small glimpse of understanding in the distance that truly was a meeting at the verge of differences.

PIONEERING THE IDEA OF VIRTUAL GATHERINGS

It is hard to believe how fast things have advanced. Long before these recognized Internet icons emerged, I was dreaming of virtual gatherings at the peril of being thought a "crazy woman." I remember my first peek into the future of such a possibility. It was 1997, when Placeware was launched as a commercial online conferencing product. It was a bit out of my league at the time as a business owner. With only dial-up available in my area, it would be a few years before I actually saw or experienced a virtual classroom. However, not being able to see it did not inhibit me in imagining its possibilities. I even remember Joel Barker and me having some magical explorations of how and what you might do, if given the opportunity sometime in the future.

Bottom line, I was fascinated by the idea of being able to be with people in conversation in this new virtual world. After years of meaningful experiences with group facilitation in physical space, this new innovation caught my pioneering spirit. That same summer, I claimed the dream while on vacation. It was a starry night out in the middle of nowhere on a houseboat. Two friends and I were dreaming big dreams for ourselves as we do regularly. One of mine was to be able to have an online classroom someday, one where I could be with people in dialogue across the world. Interestingly, after that claim was made, in what seemed a flash, myriad opportunities "popped up out of the pavement" to prepare me for what was to come. In Chapter 4, one concrete example was highlighted in the best practice story about the development in 2000 of the cross-cultural dialogue center, HP's Global eSpace, under the leadership of Dr. Sidalia Reel.

As online forums and live chat started to gain acceptance, adding still other possibilities for putting our differences to work, I decided to independently test the waters. It was January 2003. I had made a New Year's resolution to take off a few pounds, so I joined Weight Watchers Online. I had read about its message boards, where you could interact with others for support.

At first, I did what I've learned a lot of people do: lurk. After signing on, I would just hover over other people's lively conversations like I was eavesdropping, not really knowing how to begin and feeling surprisingly shy and vulnerable. It was actually a lot like life in physical space, when you show up someplace, don't know anyone, and no one notices you. I started dabbling, leaving a message here and there. Some were answered; some were ignored. I still felt disconnected, like a real outsider. Just when I was about to give up and join the naysayers of the world, questioning the value of all the fuss over virtual communication, I decided to try one more attempt.

The WB Café

One morning in February 2004, I set up my own message board at Weight Watchers. I posted a welcoming message setting up the idea of looking for "buddies" to share the journey. Within minutes, a spirited, friendly woman named Nia showed up to accept my invitation and shared her story. Soon others also came, and by the end of the day the café was full. The rest is history. The WB Café has been open 365 days a year ever since. The first person to arrive every day opens and posts the first message. The last one "takes the trash and sets for morning." There are no rules, but we've shared the leadership and ownership for this special place to meet, connect, and find support.

Like any café in your neighborhood, our virtual café has its regulars, including a retired nurse, stay-at-home moms with overwhelming schedules, a professor, hardworking professionals, a college student soon to finish graduate school, and a high school senior now soon to graduate from Columbia University. We are a cast of unique characters from all around the United States, as well as Puerto Rico, plus visitors from Canada and South Africa. Together we are about as different as you can imagine. We've found common ground around being healthy, but most of all we made friends sight unseen, voice unheard.

As I was developing the Five Distinctive Qualities of Leadership for this book, I realized that the WB Café has lived up to every one. We thrive on the diversity of our group. If you stick around, you can be sure there is a chair waiting for you with your name carved in it. If you are new, you find the warmest welcome. Our diversity makes it interesting, and we've learned together that we are a creative force. We work to get to know one another. From our unique differences come the sharing of stories, victories, heartbreaks, and the personalities that resonate through each person's writing. Personal responsibility is what has kept the café an evolving place. New ideas have refreshed its name, its welcome, and brought about positive changes we needed to bring out the best in all of us, as well as keep the benefits flowing to everyone.

It's hard not to imagine the good that would come if organizations, businesses, and all parts of society could someday enjoy the experience of a culture of inclusion like this seemingly small example suggests. I asked a few of the longtime WB Café regulars to share why they come and what the experience has meant to them:

Nia: Like ducks flying in formation, we all take our turn leading. When one of us falls behind, another takes the lead. Who would have thought that such a close-knit group would have evolved from that very first thread started years ago....

Alice Ann: We've never met face to face, but we feel a connection from inside. We supported one another through weight loss, celebrations of many kinds, and personal losses as well. We're all so different but so alike in our own special ways.

Marylynn: I've gotten more support here from this little group than any meeting. Overtime, I feel a sense of responsibility to everyone; it's part of who I am as a person. I come here because it feels like home.

Wanda: I love coming here to chat and just to be cheered up and spurred on to reach my goals. You can "'fess up" with never a fear of condemnation; we've all been in the same place. We care for one another.

Beth: I come here because I feel loved and accepted. I am always, always welcomed back. I feel a closeness to everyone; I don't need to see them or talk to them with my voice. In my mind, I visualize what everyone looks like.

Lorilynn: Some women have breezed through our lives at the café. We miss them all and "call out their names" frequently and fondly because of the ways they have all touched each and every one of our lives and made a difference to us all.

KEY POINTS: THE WB CAFÉ STORY

▶ You don't have to sit "knee to knee" or even see or hear others to appreciate their differences and create an inclusive environment. Virtual space is creating new possibilities for all of us.

▶ When you put your differences to work to cocreate, a sense of shared ownership and personal responsibility emerges that brings out everyone's ability to step up to take the lead.

▶ Rich communication sustains relationships, builds trust, and helps you get to know more about each other, appreciating each person's differences.

As we've learned through the many stories in this book, the WB Café is still another example that demonstrates the power of putting our differences to work. It was this early positive experience that gave me the courage to take a bold step in the virtual world.

Global Dialogue Center

In November 2004, my company launched the Global Dialogue Center (see the illustration), a virtual gathering place for people throughout the world with a focus on leadership, professional, and personal development. It is open to the public and fueled by the belief that if all of us can think, question, and explore new ideas together, we can become more effective leaders in our organizations, marketplaces, workplaces, communities, and with our families. In turn, this maximizes the opportunities for us to meet on common ground to put our differences to work to create a world better than we know today.

We've worked to listen to our visitors and learn with them, continuing to redefine what "virtual event" means to them. We have been blessed with

Global Dialogue Center Site Map

the finest of thought leaders, who have contributed their best work. We seemed to attract those with a pioneering spirit for the new and different. This is also reflected in a global ever-changing community of people who join us to receive their wisdom and to share themselves across the distance representing over 125 countries. Most of our contributors and members of our community have never met—physically, that is. We know their presence well, and we've witnessed their growth. It is definitely a win-win-win for everyone! Our operating model has been intentionally designed as a practice of the five distinctive qualities for putting our differences to work. The whole place is brimming with mutualism.

Working in a virtual gathering place is now my practice, including operating from my virtual office with customers in our mainstream business. It is a world that is changing rapidly with advances continuing to open up new ways for us to *be* in a community. By the way of noting the power of vision, our bank of conference rooms at Global Dialogue Center Conference Center is today powered by Microsoft Office Live Meeting®, which acquired Placeware in 2003, as I mentioned previously—the very organization that sparked my early dream. What are those chances?

In their beautiful, groundbreaking book *A Simpler Way*, Margaret Wheatley and Myron Kellner-Rogers describe clearly the experience of putting our differences to work for the first time with a new team, breaking new ground in some innovative never-done-before direction:

> Every act of organizing is an experiment. We begin with desire, with a sense of purpose and direction. But we enter the experience vulnerable, unprotected by the illusory cloak of prediction. We acknowledge that we don't know how this work will actually unfold. We discover what we are capable of as we go along. We engage with others for the experiment. We are willing to commit to a system whose effectiveness cannot be seen until it is in motion. *Every act of organizing is an act of faith.*

HP Common Thread 2.0

The following story shows how organizing was an act of faith for a small team of people-focused innovators at HP. It was the ultimate putting our differences to work project. The initial aim was to forge a new virtual path across the company, in record time, with big ambitions of creating an influential Web-subscriber-based vehicle to connect employees at all levels in a *personal way* to HP's leadership team, their culture of innovation worldwide, and their commitment to diversity and inclusion throughout the world.

The HP Common Thread core team for the mission was tiny—three, to be exact. It was headed by Barbara Hopland, then Director, Diversity Awareness Solutions, joined by Debby McIsaac, Director, Culture and Engagement, and Dee Blackwell, Diversity Project Manager. I had the privilege of being invited to team up as a creative partner, bringing my outside perspective from building the Global Dialogue Center community. Together there was an intentional blend of inside and outside differences with unique knowledge, know-how, and strengths that everyone brought to the table.

"We were able to bring an idea to life, because we ultimately respected the different set of talents that each brought," reflected Barbara Hopland. "We learned differences can cause initial conflict and sometimes misunderstanding in the midst of a lot of creative drive, especially when the pressure is on. What made it work well was that we all had the courage and conviction to mission to keep our focus on achieving results, for and through the people of HP. This brought out the best in all of us."

It was true that none of us knew exactly how the work would unfold or even how to classify what it was at first so that sponsors, leaders, and employees would grasp its value and find it personally meaningful. So for lack of a different term, we initially called it a "news digest," but as we worked in partnership with HP employees around the world, they helped everyone see it was much more.

In March 2006, HP's Common Thread was launched in partnership with HP's employees across the world, joining together to tell their stories and transfer knowledge business to business in ways never imagined. There was meaning behind the name Common Thread that resonated across the world: "The name symbolizes our undeniable link across businesses, cultures, differences, and

HP Common Thread 2.0

Employees around the world proved that Common Thread was much more than its original idea. Through their willingness to participate and share their ideas and stories, it became a:

1. virtual peer-to-peer global development experience;

2. professional and leadership development resource;

3. place for ongoing dialogue with senior leaders and HP innovators;

4. "town hall" for sharing best practices, insight, and opinion;

5. resource for outside perspectives and innovative new thinking;

6. vehicle tapping into creative ideas for responding to a dynamic marketplace;

7. virtual stage with an open mike;

8. giant blog with many contributing authors;

9. virtual gathering place.

distance. Together, we make up HP's global team. Each one of us plays an important role in our success."

In its first year, over seventy senior leaders and members of the executive team contributed personal features and offered their sponsorship and encouragement. Scores of HP employee contributors showed up, excited to share their best practices, success stories, as well as editorials on key topics, like the need to "think globally." They also coached, mentored, and worked together in virtual town halls, offering their expertise and global perspectives on a wide range of business issues. In the spirit of mutualism, the Global Dialogue Center's thought leaders brought in outside perspectives via mini podcasts, self-learning exhibits, and tips for "learning on the go" to complement Common Thread's business-focused themes, such as the power of collaboration, discovering meaning in your work, and the culture of innovation.

Common Thread today, like all of us, is continuing to adapt, change, and become more. New ideas and Web 2.0 features are opening up opportunities to again take it to a new level. The goal is for it to morph itself with the changing needs of HP and employees across the world. After the initial experience, we know the possibilities are truly limitless. At HP, Common Thread's one-year anniversary was celebrated with more than 160,000 subscribers.

Barbara Hopland, Dee Blackwell, and Debby McIsaac shared their reflections on the experiences of learning firsthand that diversity is the fastest way to innovation, leadership, and high performance:

BARBARA HOPLAND

Giving birth to Common Thread was an amazing experience. Without question, it was one of the hardest and most challenging work assignments that I ever had to tackle. Bringing new ideas to life has many twists and turns. I would have likely given up and given in to the naysayer on more than one occasion were it not for our team.

I learned that people, at all levels, are very open to and appreciate the opportunity to share their experiences and learnings. They know that these lessons translate across job functions, businesses, and languages. I still can't believe that not one person turned us down when we asked them to be a contributor. Two big lessons: First, leveraging all the dimensions of diversity in HP's family delivers remarkable results—*faster!* Second, cross-cultural diversity dramatically increases the flow of new ideas; *everyone benefits!*

I will always remember the feeling of opening up the letter from California that the team created to celebrate our first year—and seeing in print the words "HP Common Thread—Results Achieved!" on a small laminated sign. It hangs in my office and is a symbol and reminder that *anything* is possible when you believe in your idea, have a talented team, and execute with precision.

DEE BLACKWELL

It was interesting to watch how the veil of separateness was lifted, as employees reached out to connect to the larger HP community to share something that was important to them. It was amazing to witness how a novel idea for creating community became such a hub for conversation. You can't quell our human instincts to connect with one another and to want to reach out to show the best in ourselves and others given the chance.

Opening a new path with a new team is challenging with all that creative energy flowing through every step. I learned that sometimes what seems to be a breaking point actually works to be a healing start and the beginning of effective collaboration. What changed me the most is that in the churn of change, the challenge of reaching inside myself to do something never done before, and the discomfort of learning, I found a new kind of strength. It helped me reclaim my personal value, and it reignited the embers of loyalty and faith that we really do care about one another.

DEBBY McISAAC

I learned meaning really matters. We all felt early on that we were doing something very special. Something that was bigger than our job descriptions or an "action item." It was something that would be part of what we could pass on—I would call it sacred work, if I were being honest. In our core as a team, we knew that we were touching people, helping people, lifting folks up, making connections, building bridges—all kinds of things that felt *real* and *true*. We didn't need anyone else's recognition; the work and the feedback from those we served became our fuel and our inspiration to keep going. In an innovative project, learning on the go is essential. It changed us all, like we started as babies and emerged as full-grown adults, full of new experiences, perspectives, and skills. It was a great development laboratory—full of experimenting and fast-cycle continuous improvement.

What became very clear: There is no shortage of energy, ideas, or inspiration on the part of employees all around the world. They want to be connected, listened to, share their perspective, be seen, and be appreciated. People have no trouble *instantly* connecting with each other—finding all kinds of things in common—regardless of distance or difference. The work is easier and flows when you remember these things.

The experience has increased my confidence. Anything can be done—if you want to make it happen. I will remember deeply the experience and fun of working *freely* as a high-performing team. There was a joy that came from both the little victories and big milestones.

KEY POINTS: HP COMMON THREAD STORY

▶ Diversity is the key driver of success. By leveraging all the dimensions of differences—calling on everyone's strengths—remarkable results are produced *faster*!

▶ Breakthrough ideas and tangible results emerge when you meet at the verge of your differences. Trailblazers learn as they go, using every opportunity as a development laboratory.

▶ People have no trouble instantly connecting with each other regardless of difference or distance. People want to be part of endeavors that have meaning and matter; such experience fuels inspiration, new ideas, confidence, and high performance.

THE FUTURE OF VIRTUAL GATHERING

There is great promise out there for connecting in virtual space with new expanding tools to productively solve our most pressing problems, learn from one another, and bring innovations needed to create a better world for everyone. Certainly, the pioneering efforts showcased in this book—including the HP Common Thread, the Habitat JAM, the Global Innovation Outlook, the Greater IBM Connection, the WB Café, and Global Dialogue Center, and many other stories we've mentioned—prove that good things can be done through technology and that people across the world resoundingly agree that they want to know more about each other. When given the opportunity, we prove every time that it is our differences working together that create the fastest way to innovation, leadership, and high performance.

When we focus on investing our energies into influencing a positive outcome, we also work to curb limiting beliefs. The future of the Internet is largely up to us, collectively. As with any tool or other gift, we can make a conscious choice about how we use it for right or wrong. As idealistic as it may sound, if enough of us were living by the Five Distinctive Qualities of Leadership, holding personal responsibility as a core belief and mutualism as the final arbiter, we just might create the tipping point that will ensure the Internet will be good for all. *Hold that thought!*

Responsibility is the price of greatness.
—Sir Winston Churchill

A Send-off: A Final Word

send-off *n* : a celebratory demonstration of goodwill
and enthusiasm for the beginning of a new venture

From the first day I started writing this book, I've wondered who you are, what you do, where you've been—and what would be in your mind as you reached this final page. I assume you have a pioneering spirit, or you probably wouldn't have chosen this book. If you took its message all in, I hope it is because you plan to do something with it.

As I wrote in the beginning, this book is an invitation to pioneer a new era—one that will begin a long and distinct period of leadership history that brings out the best in people and affirms that the fastest way to innovation, leadership, and high performance is through putting our differences to work in ways that everyone benefits.

Wisdom that has passed the test of time has always been a reliable and inspiring force in my life, as this book reflects. Dr. Bruce Lloyd, Professor of Strategic Management at South Bank University in London, has a nice way of saying it: "Wisdom is knowledge with a long shelf-life." It always surprises me when a piece of wisdom seems to show up when I need it most. In the final days of writing, I opened one of my cherished books discovered by chance a few years ago. It is well out of print. The author, John Homer Miller, doesn't have instant name recognition today, but he was a leader with many contributions and influence in another time. The following message came from his book *Take a Second Look at Yourself*, published over fifty years ago. It speaks to what I want most to pass along to you for this send-off.

> You want [a better organization,] a better world. What you need to help make [your organization better] or to make the world better is not more education of your intellect. What you need is something spiritual and ethical added to your knowledge. You need educated

emotions and a dedicated heart. Shakespeare once said that we can always tell a wise man by the fact everything he says or does smacks of something greater than himself.... Great leaders start from within and move out.

The Five Distinctive Qualities of Leadership help each of us start from within to master putting our differences to work wherever we are. Only then can we have influence in leading others. We studied and talked about each of the qualities and highlighted them in stories throughout this book. When you now add them to what you already know and practice, they create the basis for leading with a pioneering spirit enriched with a new focus on integrity and a dedicated heart necessary to draw people together and bring out the best in them. You won't be alone. The best leaders have always found new and different ways to connect and inspire individual greatness in others that brings new innovation to the world. This is our time.

Until our paths cross again...

Welcome the unexpected.

Watch for the uncharted path that bears your name.

Look for the signs that lead to the verge of differences.

I'll meet you there. Lead the way!

Resources and Studies

The following resources and studies are provided to support your work and expand your own learning and discovery about putting our differences to work.

Putting Our Differences to Work
Resource Center

This is the author's online interactive Web 2.0 site created to support your work, including direct access to resources and tools listed here, live chat opportunities with Debbe Kennedy, events, podcasts, blog, and additional resources.

www.puttingourdifferencestowork.com

Putting Our Differences to Work
Organizational Snapshot

Access to the online version or downloadable PDF worksheets.

www.puttingourdifferencestowork.com/snapshot

The Wisdom Collection Directory

Putting Our Differences to Work holds a treasury of wisdom that has been woven into each of its chapters. The *Wisdom Collection Directory* was created to give you easy access to the references in the book all in one place, including knowledge, stories, thoughts, and quotes from a diverse group of leaders, past and present, from public, private, corporate, and government organizations; entrepreneurs; educators; and global citizens with finger-prints from authors, philosophers, experts, artists, poets and musicians.

www.puttingourdifferencestowork.com

Global Dialogue Center

A virtual gathering place for people throughout the world with an intentional focus on leadership, professional, and personal development. It is also the home of Women in the Lead.

www.globaldialoguecenter.com

- ► **Putting Our Differences to Work Blog**
  www.globaldialoguecenter.blogs.com/differences

- ► **Moments of Insights Collection**
  www.globaldialoguecenter.com/insights

- ► **Working Together with Debbe Kennedy**
  www.globaldialoguecenter.com/workingtogether

- ► **Women in the Lead: A Unique Online Resource Center**
  www.globaldialoguecenter.com/women

- ► **Women's Gallery at Women in the Lead**
  www.globaldialoguecenter.com/women/gallery.shtml

- ► **Knowledge Gallery**
  www.globaldialoguecenter.com/exhibits

- ► **Work and Life with a Disability with Bill Tipton**
  www.globaldialoguecenter.blogs.com/disabilities

- ► **The Meaning Difference Blog with author Dr. Alex Pattakos**
  www.globaldialoguecenter.blogs.com/meaning

PODCASTS, VIDEOS, AND EXHIBITS

Related Videos and Tools from Joel Barker

Joel Barker has an extensive library of videos and other useful tools for putting our differences to work. Here are a few that will support you in all the phases of change:

- ► *Innovation at the Verge*   Joel explores the ideas and discoveries he introduces in *Putting Our Differences to Work* about innovation at the verge of differences. In this landmark film, he reads from *Putting Our Differences to Work* by Debbe Kennedy.

- ► *Wealth, Innovation and Diversity: Putting Our Differences to Work in the 21st Century* Joel discusses the connection between diversity and innovation and between innovation and wealth.

- ► *Power of Vision* The *Power of Vision* demonstrates that having a positive vision of the future is the most forceful motivator for change—for success—that companies, schools, communities, nations, and individuals possess.

- ► *Paradigm Pioneers* *Paradigm Pioneers* identifies the essential traits of these trailblazers and discusses how you can become one.

- ► *Leadershift: Five Lessons for Leaders in the 21st Century* The concept of leadership is changing. *Leadershift* explores these shifts and offers five concepts to improve the performance of any leader.

- ► *The New Business of Paradigms* Organizations need to innovate and change in order to survive. Joel's best-selling training video, *The New Business of Paradigms*, explains how the rules we live by can limit our ability to innovate and be creative.

All are available through Star Thrower Distribution: www.starthrower.com/joel_barker.htm; (800) 242-3220.

Implications Wheel

A strategic tool for exploring the future and long-term implications of change.

www.implicationswheel.com

Seeds of Innovation Team and Organization Assessment

This assessment, created by Elaine Dundon and Alex Pattakos, Ph.D., allows individuals and teams to identify where new ideas and processes are thriving and what's standing in the way. Available through HRDQ.

www.seedsofinnovation.com

RELATED STUDIES

The direct online links to the studies, if applicable, are available at www.puttingourdifferencestowork.com. Each provides a unique perspective on changing workplaces, marketplaces, and communities and the opportunities we have to put our differences to work.

- ▶ "Diversity and Community in the Twenty-first Century: The 2006 Johan Skytte Prize Lecture," by Robert D. Putnam, Nordic Political Science Association, 2007

- ▶ *Global CEO Study: Expanding the Innovation Horizon*, IBM, 2006

- ▶ *Global Innovation Outlook 2.0 Report*, IBM Global Services, 2006

- ▶ How to Use Social Media to Engage Employees, Global Survey by Melcrum, 2007

- ▶ "Identity Integration and Innovation," by Chi-Ying Cheng, Jeffrey Sanchez-Burks, and Fiona Lee, Ross School of Business, March 2007

- ▶ *The Future of the Internet II: Survey of Technology Thinkers and Stakeholders*, by Pew Internet & American Life Project, September 2006

- ▶ "Building Social and Intellectual Capital: HR's Contribution to Organizational Effectiveness," by Robert J. Green, Society of Human Resource Management (SHRM), June 2007

- ▶ *Research on Managing Groups and Teams*, volume 10, *Affect and Groups*, by Elizabeth A. Mannix, Margaret A. Neale, and Cameron P. Anderson

Notes and Sources

The following books and other resources have provided information, fostered ideas, and been a continuous source of inspiration for this work. I am grateful to these messengers.

Introduction

The Conference Board. Press releases, "Top 10 Challenges Overall"; "Top 10 Challenges, Regional Comparison Table," October 4, 2007.

Microsoft Office Live Meeting® Leadership Forum. "How to Get Buy-in for New Ideas," with Debbe Kennedy, 2005.

PART 1

Chapter 1

Arrien, Angeles. *Sign of Life: The Five Universal Shapes and How to Use Them.* New York: Tarcher, 1998.

Barker, Joel A. *Five Regions of the Future: Preparing Your Business for Tomorrow's Technology Revolution.* New York: Penguin, 2005.

———. *Paradigms: The Business of Discovering the Future.* New York: Collins, 1993.

———. *Wealth, Innovation and Diversity.* Video. Star Thrower Distribution, www.starthrower.com, (800) 242-3220.

Collins, Jim. *Good to Great: Why Some Companies Make the Leap and Others Don't.* New York: HarperBusiness, 2001.

Dundon, Elaine. *The Seeds of Innovation: Cultivating the Synergy That Fosters New Ideas.* New York: AMACOM, 2002.

George, Michael L., James Works, and Kimberly Watson-Hemphill. *Fast Innovation: Achieving Superior Differentiation, Speed to Market, and Increased Profitability.* New York: McGraw-Hill, 2005.

Global Dialogue Center. "We Came to the Habitat JAM" Knowledge Gallery exhibit, www.globaldialoguecenter.com/habitatjam.

Goldsmith, Marshall, Cathy L. Greenberg, Alastair Robertson, and Maya Hu-Chan. *Global Leadership: The Next Generation.* New York: FT Press, 2003 (summary quote on p. 5).

IBM. *Global CEO Study 2006—Expanding the Innovation Horizon.* Armonk, NY: Author, 2006.

———. "Innovation Opens Up: IBM's Global Innovation Outlook—Identifying and Harnessing Innovation Opportunities and Enabling the Collaborations That Matter." *Global Innovation Outlook 2.0.* Armonk, NY: Author.

Johansson, Frans. *The Medici Effect: What Elephants and Epidemics Can Teach Us about Innovation.* Cambridge, MA: Harvard Business School Press, 2006.

Krueger, Jerry, and Emily Killham. "Who's Driving Innovation at Your Company?" *Gallup Management Journal,* September 2006.

"Leading Change When Business Is Good: An Interview with Samuel J. Palmisano." *Harvard Business Review,* reprint R0412C.

Mannix, Elizabeth A., Margaret A. Neale, and Cameron P. Anderson. *Research on Managing Groups and Teams: Vol. 10. Affect and Groups.* Burlington, MA: Elsevier, 2007.

Patel, Hitendra, and Holger Koehler. *Cementing Innovation: You Don't Have to Be High-Tech to Innovate—Just High-Touch.* Cambridge, MA: Innovation Management, n.d. www.innovation-management.com/downloads/Cementing_Innovation.Final.pdf.

Patel, Hitendra, Steve Wyatt, and Arun Mahizhnan. "Make Innovation a National Imperative." IPS-Monitor Business Times Innovation Series, article 6, www.monitor.com.

Putnam, Robert D. "Diversity and Community in the Twenty-first Century: The 2006 Johan Skytte Prize Lecture." *Nordic Political Science Association Journal,* June 2007.

Putnam, Robert D., and Lewis M. Feldstein. *Better Together: Restoring the American Community.* New York: Simon & Schuster, 2003. www.bettertogether.org.

Chapter 2

Drucker, Peter F. *The Daily Drucker.* New York: Harper, 2004.

Inamori, Kazuo. *For People and for Profit: A Business Philosophy for the 21st Century.* Tokyo: Kodansha International, 1997.

Kennedy, Debbe. *Action Dialogues: Meaningful Conversations to Accelerate Change.* Foreword by Frances Hesselbein. San Francisco: Berrett-Koehler, 2000.

Miller, John Homer. *Take a Look at Yourself.* Nashville, TN: Abingdon-Cokesbury, 1953 (p. 59 for the story of Abraham Lincoln).

Chapter 3

Arrien, Angeles. *Sign of Life.* Tarcher 1998.

Humes, James. *Churchill: Speaker of the Century.* New York: Stein & Day 1980.

Kennedy, Debbe. *Diversity Breakthrough!* Strategic Action Series. San Francisco: Berrett-Koehler, 2000.

———. "Our Dreams in Action." Poem. 1990.

PART 2

Chapter 4

Block, Peter. *Stewardship: Choosing Service over Self-Interest.* San Francisco: Berrett-Koehler, 1993.

Charan, Ram. *Know-How: Eight Skills That Separate People Who Perform and Those Who Don't.* New York: Crown Business, 2007.

Cox, Taylor, Jr., and Ruby L. Beale. *Cultural Diversity in Organizations: Theory, Research, and Practice.* San Francisco: Berrett-Koehler, 1994.

————. *Developing Competency to Manage Diversity: Readings, Cases, and Activities.* San Francisco: Berrett-Koehler, 1997.

Drucker, Peter F. *Management Challenges for the 21st Century.* New York: Harper-Collins, 1999.

————. *Management: Tasks, Responsibilities, Practices.* New York: Harper & Row, 1974.

Gandhi, Mahatma. *All Men Are Brothers: Autobiographical Reflections.* Comp. and ed. Krishna Kripalani. New York: Continuum, 1999.

Greater IBM Connection. www.ibm.com/ibm/greateribm.

Heider, John. *The Tao of Leadership: Lao Tzu's Tao Te Ching Adapted for a New Age.* New York: Humanics, 1997.

Hesselbein, Frances. "If They Look at Us, Will They See Themselves?" *Leader to Leader* (a publication of the Drucker Foundation and Jossey-Bass Publishers), 11 (Winter 1999).

————. *Hesselbein on Leadership.* San Francisco: Jossey-Bass, 2002.

————. *Confidence: How Winning Streaks and Losing Streaks Begin and End.* New York: Crown Business, 2004.

————. *World Class: Thriving Locally in the Global Economy.* New York: Simon & Schuster, 1995.

Kennedy, Debbe. *Breakthrough! Everything You Need to Start a Solution Revolution.* Montara, CA: Leadership Solutions Publishing, 1998.

Mannix, Elizabeth A., and Margaret A. Neale. "Diversity at Work: Diversity in Employee Teams Does Not Always Equal Superior Performance." *Scientific American Mind,* August–September 2006.

Stern, Gary J. *The Drucker Foundation Self-Assessment Tool: Process Guide and Workbook.* New York: Drucker Foundation; San Francisco: Jossey-Bass, 1998. www.pfdf.org.

Chapter 5

Barker, Joel A. *Paradigm Pioneers.* Video. Star Thrower Distribution, www.starthrower.com, (800) 242-3220.

————. *Wealth, Innovation and Diversity.* Video. Star Thrower Distribution, www.starthrower.com, (800) 242-3220.

Bland, J. "About Gender: Differences." www.gender.org/about/00_diffs.htm.

Block, Peter. *Stewardship: Choosing Service over Self-Interest.* San Francisco: Berrett-Koehler, 1993.

Coffman, Curt, and Gabriel Gonzalez-Molina. "Steering toward Engagement." In *Follow This Path: How the World's Greatest Organizations Drive Growth by Unleashing Human Potential.* New York: Warner, 2002.

Cox, Taylor, Jr., and Ruby L. Beale. *Cultural Diversity in Organizations: Theory, Research, and Practice*. San Francisco: Berrett-Koehler, 1994.

————. *Developing Competency to Manage Diversity: Readings, Cases, and Activities*. San Francisco: Berrett-Koehler, 1997.

Cranfield School of Management. "The Case Against," Andrew Kakabadse; "The Case For," Susan Vinnicombe. *Management Focus* 12 (Summer 1999): 1–5.

Drucker, Peter F. *Management: Tasks, Responsibilities, Practices*. New York: Harper & Row, 1974.

Easwaran, Ekanth. *Gandhi, the Man: The Story of His Transformation*. Tomales, CA: Nilgiri, 1997.

Ellinor, Linda, and Glenna Gerard. Dialogue: *Rediscover the Transforming Power of Conversation*. New York: Wiley, 1998.

Fisher, Helen. *The First Sex: The Natural Talents of Women and How They Are Changing the World*. New York: Ballantine Books, 1999.

Hesselbein, Frances. "The Key to Cultural Transformation." *Leader to Leader* (a publication of the Drucker Foundation and Jossey-Bass Publishers), 12 (Spring 1999).

Inamori, Kazuo. *A Passion for Success: Practical, Inspirational and Spiritual Insight from Japan's Leading Entrepreneur*. New York: McGraw-Hill, 2007.

Jackson, Shirley Ann. "Powering Innovation through Diversity." Speech delivered at IBM Watson Research Labs, October 30, 2006.

Kanter, Rosabeth Moss. "Collaborative Advantage: The Art of Alliances." *Harvard Business Review*, August 1994, reprint 94405. Kennedy, Debbe. *Breakthrough! Everything You Need to Start a Solution Revolution*. Montara, CA: Leadership Solutions Publishing, 1998.

Ladies Room. "Gender Differences in Communication." 2006. www.geocities.com/ Wellesley/2052/genddiff.html.

Shaffer, Carolyn R., and Kristen Anundsen. *Creating Community Anywhere: Finding Support and Connection in a Fragmented World*. New York: Tarcher/Putnam, 1993.

Shirley, Donna. *Managing Martians*. New York: Broadway Books, 1998.

Some, Malidoma Patrice. *The Healing Wisdom of Africa: Finding Life Purpose through Nature, Ritual and Community*. New York: Tarcher/Putnam, 1998.

Roosevelt, Thomas R., Jr. *Redefining Diversity*. New York: American Management Association, 1996.

Turner, Robin. "Male Logic" and "Woman's Intuition." *Sensible Marks of Ideas: Phi* (1997). http://neptune.spaceports.com/~words/malelogic.html.

————. *A Meeting of Minds: A Brief Rhetoric for Writers and Readers*. New York: Longman, 2004.

Chapter 6

Arrien, Angeles, ed. *Working Together: Producing Synergy by Honoring Diversity*. New York: New Leaders Press, 1998.

Barker, Joel A. *Paradigm Pioneers*. Video. Star Thrower Distribution, www.star thrower.com, (800) 242-3220.

————. *Wealth, Innovation and Diversity*. Video. Star Thrower Distribution, www .starthrower.com, (800) 242-3220.

Block, Peter. *Stewardship: Choosing Service over Self-Interest.* San Francisco: Berrett-Koehler, 1993.

Cox, Taylor, Jr., and Ruby L. Beale. *Cultural Diversity in Organizations: Theory, Research, and Practice.* San Francisco: Berrett-Koehler, 1994.

———. *Developing Competency to Manage Diversity: Readings, Cases, and Activities.* San Francisco: Berrett-Koehler, 1997.

Dessler, Gary. "How to Earn Your Employees' Commitment." *Academy of Management Executive* 13, no. 2 (May 1999): 58–67 (citing the Saturn employee survey).

Drucker, Peter F. *Management: Tasks, Responsibilities, Practices.* New York: Harper & Row, 1974.

Hesselbein, Frances. "If They Look at Us, Will They See Themselves?" *Leader to Leader* (a publication of the Drucker Foundation and Jossey-Bass Publishers), 11 (Winter 1999).

Inamori, Kazuo. *For People and for Profit: A Business Philosophy for the 21st Century.* Trans. T. R. Reid. Tokyo: Kodansha International, 1997.

———. *A Passion for Success.* New York: McGraw-Hill, 1995; new edition 2007.

Kanter, Rosabeth Moss. *Change Masters: Corporate Entrepreneurs at Work.* New York: International Thomson Business Press, 1992.

Kennedy, Debbe. *Breakthrough! Everything You Need to Start a Solution Revolution.* Montara, CA: Leadership Solutions, 1998.

Luhabe, Wendy. *Defining Moments: Experiences of Black Executives in South Africa's Workplace.* Pietermaritzburg: University of Natal Press, 2002.

Mandela, Nelson. *Long Walk to Freedom.* New York: Little, Brown, 1995 (p. 625).

Melcrum. "How to Use Social Media to Engage Employees." 2007. www.melcrum.com.

Nicholson, Peter J. "Harnessing the Wisdom of Crowds: The New Contours of Intellectual Authority." Speech delivered to the Fields Institute for Research in Mathematical Sciences, June 2006.

Stayer, Ralph. "How I Learned to Let My Workers Lead." *Harvard Business Review*, reprint 90610, OnPoint December 2001, product 8318.

Surowiecki, James. *The Wisdom of Crowds.* New York: Anchor Books, 2005.

Wheatley, Margaret J. *Turning to One Another: Simple Conversations to Restore Hope to the Future.* San Francisco: Berrett-Koehler, 2002.

Chapter 7

Barker, Joel A. *Wealth, Innovation and Diversity.* Video. Star Thrower Distribution, www.starthrower.com, (800) 242-3220.

Boss, Shira. "Even in a Virtual World, 'Stuff' Matters." *New York Times*, September 9, 2007.

"Brave Heart: Hope for All Mankind" exhibit at the Knowledge Gallery, Global Dialogue Center, www.globaldialoguecenter.com/braveheart.

Cox, Taylor, Jr., and Ruby L. Beale. *Cultural Diversity in Organizations: Theory, Research, and Practice.* San Francisco: Berrett-Koehler, 1994.

———. *Developing Competency to Manage Diversity: Readings, Cases, and Activities.* San Francisco: Berrett-Koehler, 1997.

Drucker, Peter F. "Managing Oneself." *Harvard Business Review*, January 2005, HBR Classic reprint R0501K.

Ellinor, Linda, and Glenna Gerard. *Dialogue: Rediscover the Transforming Power of Conversation*. New York: Wiley, 1998.

Frankl, Viktor E. *Man's Search for Meaning*. Boston: Beacon, 2006.

Global Dialogue Center. "Discovering Deeper Meaning." Moments of Insight Collection, www.globaldialoguecenter.com/insights-alexpattakos

Huang, Chungliang Al, and Jerry Lynch. *Mentoring: The Tao of Giving and Receiving Wisdom*. San Francisco: HarperSanFrancisco, 1995.

Katzenbach, Jon R., and Douglas K. Smith. *The Wisdom of Teams: Creating the High-Performance Organization*. Cambridge, MA: Harvard Business School Press, 1992.

Kennedy, Debbe. *Breakthrough! Everything You Need to Start a Solution Revolution*. Montara, CA: Leadership Solutions, 1998.

Leavitt, Harold J., and Jean Lipman-Blumen. "Hot Groups." *Harvard Business Review*, July 1, 1995, reprint 95404.

O'Neil, John. *Leadership Aikido: 6 Business Practices to Turn around Your Life*. New York: Three Rivers Press, 1997.

Pasternak, Jeff. "Brave Heart." *Double Cover* album, www.pasternakmusic.com.

Pattakos, Alex. *Prisoners of Our Thoughts: Viktor Frankl's Principles for Discovering Meaning in Life and Work*. San Francisco: Berrett-Koehler, 2004, www.prisonersofourthoughts.com.

Pfeffer, Jeffrey, and John F. Veiga, "Putting People First for Organizational Success." *Academy of Management Executive* 13, no. 2 (May 1999): 37–48.

Shaffer, Carolyn R., and Kristen Anundsen. *Creating Community Anywhere: Finding Support and Connection in a Fragmented World*. New York: Tarcher/Putnam, 1993.

Chapter 8

Barker, Joel A. *Paradigm Pioneers*. Video. Star Thrower Distribution, www.starthrower.com, (800) 242-3220.

———. *Wealth, Innovation and Diversity*. Video. Star Thrower Distribution, www.starthrower.com, (800) 242-3220.

Bristol, Claude M. *The Magic of Believing*. New York: Pocket Books, 1991.

Carr-Ruffino, Norma. *Diversity Success Strategies*. Burlington, MA: Butterworth-Heinemann, 1999.

Cox, Taylor, Jr., and Ruby L. Beale. *Cultural Diversity in Organizations: Theory, Research & Practice*. San Francisco: Berrett-Koehler, 1994.

———. *Developing Competency to Manage Diversity: Readings, Cases, and Activities*. San Francisco: Berrett-Koehler, 1997.

Ellinor, Linda, and Glenna Gerard. *Dialogue: Rediscover the Transforming Power of Conversation*. New York: Wiley, 1998.

Emmons, Robert A. *Thanks! How the New Science of Gratitude Can Make You Happier*. New York: Houghton Mifflin, 2007.

Fortune. "Where Diversity Really Works." July 19, 1999.

Hammonds, Keith H. "Difference Is Power." *Fast Company*, August 2002 (profiling J. T. [Ted] Childs Jr.).

Hateley, Barbara, and Warren H. Schmidt. *A Peacock in the Land of Penguins: A Tale of Diversity and Discovery*. San Francisco: Berrett-Koehler, 1997.

Hesselbein, Frances. "If They Look at Us, Will They See Themselves?" *Leader to Leader* (a publication of the Drucker Foundation and Jossey-Bass Publishers), 11 (Winter 1999).

Huang, Chungliang Al, and Jerry Lynch. *Mentoring: The Tao of Giving and Receiving Wisdom*. San Francisco: HarperSanFrancisco, 1995.

Inamori, Kazuo. *Passion for Success: Practical, Inspirational, and Spiritual Insight from Japan's Leading Entrepreneur*. New York: McGraw-Hill, 1995.

Mandela, Nelson. *Long Walk to Freedom: The Autobiography of Nelson Mandela*. New York: Little, Brown, 1995 (quote cited is on p. 625).

Miller, John Homer. *Take a Look at Yourself*. Nashville, TN: Abingdon-Cokesbury, 1953 (story of Helen Keller is on p. 81).

Shaffer, Carolyn R., and Kristen Anundsen. *Creating Community Anywhere: Finding Support and Connection in a Fragmented World*. New York: Tarcher/Putnam, 1993.

Chapter 9

Barker, Joel A. *Paradigm Pioneers*. Video. Star Thrower Distribution, www.starthrower.com, (800) 242-3220.

———. *Wealth, Innovation and Diversity*. Video. Star Thrower Distribution, www.starthrower.com, (800) 242-3220.

"The Better Future." Moments of Insight Collection at the Global Dialogue Center, www.globaldialoguecenter.com/insights-johnrenesch.

Bristol, Claude M. *The Magic of Believing*. New York: Pocket Books, 1991.

Collins, James C., and Jerry I. Porras. *Built to Last: Successful Habits of Visionary Companies*. New York: HarperBusiness, 1994.

Cox, Taylor, Jr., and Ruby L. Beale. *Developing Competency to Manage Diversity: Readings, Cases & Activities*. San Francisco: Berrett-Koehler, 1997.

———. *Cultural Diversity in Organizations: Theory, Research, and Practice*. San Francisco: Berrett-Koehler, 1994.

Dessler, Gary. "How to Earn Your Employees' Commitment." *Academy of Management Executive* 13, no. 2 (May 1999): 58–67.

Ellinor, Linda, and Glenna Gerard. *Dialogue: Rediscover the Transforming Power of Conversation*. New York: Wiley, 1998.

Hesselbein, Frances. "If They Look at Us, Will They See Themselves?" *Leader to Leader* (a publication of the Drucker Foundation and Jossey-Bass Publishers), 11 (Winter 1999).

IBM. *Thirty Years of Management Briefings, 1958–1988*. Armonk, NY: Author, 1988.

Inamori, Kazuo. *Passion for Success: Practical, Inspirational, and Spiritual Insight from Japan's Leading Entrepreneur*. New York: McGraw-Hill, 1995. New edition 2007.

Pfeffer, Jeffrey, and John F. Veiga. "Putting People First for Organizational Success." *Academy of Management Executive* 13, no. 2 (May 1999): 37–48.

"Q&A: James Surowiecki." *Forbes*, CEO Network Chat, June 1, 2004.

Renesch, John. *Getting to the Better Future: A Matter of Conscious Choosing*. San Francisco: New Business Books, 2005 (quote cited also appears in "The Conscious Organization: Workplace for the Self-Actualized," www.renesch.com/conso.html).

Salwak, Dale. *The Wonders of Solitude: Classic Wisdom*. New York: New World Library, 1995.

Surowiecki, James. *The Wisdom of Crowds*. New York: Anchor Books, 2005.

PART 3

Chapters 10–12

Boorstin, Daniel J. *The Seekers: The Story of Man's Continuous Quest to Understand His World*. Random House, 1998.

Microsoft Office Live Meeting® Leadership Forum. "How to Get Buy-in for New Ideas," with Debbe Kennedy, 2005.

Pew Internet and American Life Project. "The Future of the Internet II: Survey of Technology Thinkers and Stakeholders." Janna Quitney Anderson, Elon University, Lee Rainie, director, September 2006.

Summerfield, Brian. "Social Networking Blurs Boundaries of Learning." Executive Briefings, *Chief Learning Officer*, www.clomedia.com, October 3, 2007.

Wheatley, Margaret J., and Myron Kellner-Rogers. *A Simpler Way*. San Francisco: Berrett-Koehler, 1996.

A Send-off

Miller, John Homer. *Take a Look at Yourself*. Nashville, TN: Abingdon-Cokesbury, 1953.

Acknowledgments

I feel blessed to have had the privilege to write this book at this moment in history. As I mentioned in the beginning, this book has many fingerprints on it just the way I dreamed it would. Some are visible and others are invisible, but their influence and energy are on its pages.

First, I am deeply grateful to Sally K. Green, painter and graphic artist, founding vice president of the Global Dialogue Center and Leadership Solutions Companies, and, most of all, my cherished best friend since we were thirteen. It would be impossible to capture her many contributions to this work and to my life, but let me share a few. She contributed the beautiful cover design and artwork to bring a new symbol of innovation to life that reflects all our differences. She also brought my words and concepts to life in the graphic illustrations throughout this book as she's been magically doing since we began putting our differences to work in 1990. She has also been a creative collaborator and spent countless hours listening and encouraging me at every turn.

Joel Barker has been a teacher, mentor, and collaborative pioneer for over fifteen years. Our journeys to the verge of our differences have advanced our study and practice of putting our differences to work in ways that are difficult to recount. We promised to again meet at the verge, and it has been a miraculous "magic carpet ride." I am very grateful for his influence, collaboration, friendship, and pioneering spirit.

Our Global Dialogue Center community has broadened my beliefs in what is possible in virtual space. I express special thanks to *New York Times* best-selling author John Perkins for his inspiration and constant encouragement to the world to do our part to create a better world than we know today. To the pioneering spirits who showed up to support our dream with your talent—Alex Pattakos, Maureen Simon, Oguchi Nkwocha, John Renesch, and Joshua Peace Seeker Hughes, who have given immeasurably and believed in putting our differences to work from the start.

This book wouldn't have happened without the individual leaders who contributed and trusted me to share their stories and insights to help others. To my longtime mentor, Frances Hesselbein: I am grateful for your belief in me and all you've taught me by your leadership example. To the Habitat JAM visionaries who proved the premise of this book by giving the world a firsthand experience: Charles Kelly, Anna Tibaijuka, Mike Wing, and Gayle Moss. I extend a special thank-you to Emily Duncan, Debby McIsaac, Barbara Hopland, Dee Blackwell, Sid Reel, Paul Schoemaker, Bill Tipton, and Cindy Stanphill, who have left a legacy of achievements blazing the way for others across the world at HP. With appreciation to The Very Reverend Alan Jones, J. T. (Ted) Childs Jr., Sue Swenson, Flor Estevez, Jerrold Tucker, Yehuda Stolov, Jan Swicord, Catherine DeVrye, Wendy Luhabe, Charles Blodgett, Donna Shirley, Nana Luz, my Good Neighbor Group, and my buddies at the WB Café.

The Berrett-Koehler team has performed the miracles that made this all happen and demonstrated creativity, commitment, and care for every detail. My deepest thanks to Steve Piersanti for his belief in me and the work and for all he taught me in the process. A special thanks to Jeevan Sivasubramaniam for seeing the promise in my idea—and to Dianne Platner, Rick Wilson, Aline Magee, Michael Bass, and Laura Larson for bringing words and beauty together in a business book. And to my reviewers—Jeff Kulick, Susie Seefelt Lesieutre, and Ponn Sabra—for stretching and refining my ideas with yours—and to Barbara Clay for putting her fingerprints on this work from Australia, proposing the winning subtitle for the book.

This book emerged from a lifetime of influences that can't be overlooked. The early seeds were planted by Debby McRock and Lane Michel, my "mutual mentors." The dreams for diversity and inclusion were built on a houseboat out in the middle of nowhere with Sally and Emily. I remain deeply grateful to IBM for the value-based foundation and leadership opportunity that have had a profound influence on my life and work then and now—and to Lucille Grant for years of listening and believing in what is possible. I also express my appreciation to Judy Liljenwall for giving us our first break at HP that opened the way and to Charles Decker for the seeds you helped me plant in this meaningful space years ago that are now are blossoming.

My deepest appreciation to Melynda, Karla, Kathleen, Betsy, and Jason, for your love and support and belief in me—and to my big brother, Dr. Irving W. DeVoe, for instilling in me a high regard for excellence.

Index

About the Author

Debbe Kennedy is a master problem solver; author; virtual speaker; and founder, president, and CEO of the Leadership Solutions Companies, an award-winning women-owned enterprise since 1990, specializing in custom leadership, organizational, and virtual communications solutions. She is a pioneer and innovator in people-focused leadership–employee communications in virtual space, including creative uses of Web 2.0 technologies, and other social media.

In 2004, Debbe launched Leadership Solutions Companies' first online entity, the Global Dialogue Center. This virtual gathering place for people throughout the world has an intentional focus on leadership, professional, and personal development. The Global Dialogue Center's commitment to expanding opportunities for inclusion throughout the world for all people, with a special focus on bringing its brand of excellence to women's personal and professional development, leadership, and mentoring, was the inspiration behind the 2005 addition of Women in the Lead, a unique resource center for women worldwide.

Debbe knows the leader's journey. She has experienced it as a successful entrepreneur, a change-leading strategic partner for Fortune 100 executives and managers, a pioneer of working in virtual space, and in a distinguished leadership career with IBM Corporation for over twenty years. Her work and leadership influence have contributed to communications solutions for senior management across many corporate functions, including employee communications, marketing, professional services, diversity and inclusion, culture, employee engagement, business ethics and policy development, women's issues, management development, employee development, human resources, strategic planning and implementation. Debbe is the author of *Breakthrough! The Problem-Solving Advantage: Everything You Need to Start a Solution Revolution.*

Learn more by visiting these sites:

www.puttingourdifferencestowork.com

www.globaldialoguecenter.com

www.lscompanies.com

ABOUT BERRETT-KOEHLER PUBLISHERS

Berrett-Koehler is an independent publisher dedicated to an ambitious mission: Creating a World That Works for All.

We believe that to truly create a better world, action is needed at all levels—individual, organizational, and societal. At the individual level, our publications help people align their lives with their values and with their aspirations for a better world. At the organizational level, our publications promote progressive leadership and management practices, socially responsible approaches to business, and humane and effective organizations. At the societal level, our publications advance social and economic justice, shared prosperity, sustainability, and new solutions to national and global issues.

A major theme of our publications is "Opening Up New Space." They challenge conventional thinking, introduce new ideas, and foster positive change. Their common quest is changing the underlying beliefs, mindsets, institutions, and structures that keep generating the same cycles of problems, no matter who our leaders are or what improvement programs we adopt.

We strive to practice what we preach—to operate our publishing company in line with the ideas in our books. At the core of our approach is stewardship, which we define as a deep sense of responsibility to administer the company for the benefit of all of our "stakeholder" groups: authors, customers, employees, investors, service providers, and the communities and environment around us.

We are grateful to the thousands of readers, authors, and other friends of the company who consider themselves to be part of the "BK Community." We hope that you, too, will join us in our mission.

BE CONNECTED

Visit Our Website

Go to www.bkconnection.com to read exclusive previews and excerpts of new books, find detailed information on all Berrett-Koehler titles and authors, browse subject-area libraries of books, and get special discounts.

Subscribe to Our Free E-Newsletter

Be the first to hear about new publications, special discount offers, exclusive articles, news about bestsellers, and more! Get on the list for our free e-newsletter by going to www.bkconnection.com.

Get Quantity Discounts

Berrett-Koehler books are available at quantity discounts for orders of ten or more copies. Please call us toll-free at (800) 929-2929 or email us at bkp.orders@aidcvt.com.

Host a Reading Group

For tips on how to form and carry on a book reading group in your workplace or community, see our website at www.bkconnection.com.

Join the BK Community

Thousands of readers of our books have become part of the "BK Community" by participating in events featuring our authors, reviewing draft manuscripts of forthcoming books, spreading the word about their favorite books, and supporting our publishing program in other ways. If you would like to join the BK Community, please contact us at bkcommunity@bkpub.com.